CATHOLIC
SACRAMENTS

CATHOLIC SACRAMENTS

✝

A RICH SOURCE OF BLESSINGS

EDITED BY
JOHN F. BALDOVIN, SJ, AND
DAVID FARINA TURNBLOOM

Paulist Press
New York / Mahwah, NJ

Cover image: Baptism of the Lord—Used with Permission, Copyright 2003, John Nava/The Cathedral of Our Lady of the Angels
Cover design by Phyllis Campos
Book design by Sharyn Banks

Library of Congress Cataloging-in-Publication Data

Catholic sacraments : a rich source of blessing / edited by John F. Baldovin, S.J. and David Farina Turnbloom.
     pages cm
     Includes bibliographical references.
     ISBN 978-0-8091-4952-0 (pbk. : alk. paper) — ISBN 978-1-58768-551-4
     1. Sacraments—Catholic Church. 2. Catholic Church—Doctrines. I. Baldovin, John F. (John Francis), 1947- editor.
     BX2200.C36 2015
     234`.16088282—dc23
                                                                    2015009278

ISBN 978-0-8091-4952-0 (paperback)
ISBN 978-1-58768-551-4 (e-book)

Published by Paulist Press
997 Macarthur Boulevard
Mahwah, New Jersey 07430

www.paulistpress.com

Printed and bound in the
United States of America

Contents

5. Infant Baptism and Adult Faith –
   Michael Drumm 33

CONVERSATION QUESTIONS 37

CONFIRMATION 39
From the *Catechism of the Catholic Church* 39
Rite of Confirmation within Mass 40

6. The Missionary Nature of Confirmation –
   Marc B. Caron 42

7. Anointed to Proclaim the Kingdom –
   Liam Bergin 46

CONVERSATION QUESTIONS 49

EUCHARIST 51
From the *Catechism of the Catholic Church* 51
The Liturgy of the Eucharist 52

8. Eucharist: The Many-Faceted Jewel –
   John F. Baldovin, SJ 56

9. Being Kept by the Eucharist –
   Cardinal Seán Patrick O'Malley, OFM Cap 60

10. The Ministries of the Eucharist –
    Joyce Ann Zimmerman, CPPS 65

11. The Word in Worship –
    Kathleen Hughes, RSCJ 71

12. Sacramental Real Presence – *Rodica Stoicoiu* ..77

13. The Eucharist and Sacrifice – *Chelsea King* 82

Contents

PREFACE ix

PART ONE: WHY THE SACRAMENTS? 1

From the *Catechism of the Catholic Church* 3

   1. Catholics: A Sacramental People –
      John F. Baldovin, SJ 5

   2. What Makes Us Catholic? –
      Thomas H. Groome 8

CONVERSATION QUESTIONS 12

PART TWO: SACRAMENTS OF INITIATION......13

From the *Catechism of the Catholic Church* 15

   3. A Rite of Passage – *Aidan J. Kavanagh, OSB*....16

CONVERSATION QUESTIONS 21

BAPTISM...23

From the *Catechism of the Catholic Church* 23

Blessing and Invocation of God over Baptismal Water
(Form A)..24

   4. Baptizing a Child – *Mary Ann Clarahan*..........27

Contents

14. The Feast of Corpus Christi –
Mark Ravizza, SJ 85
CONVERSATION QUESTIONS 90

PART THREE: SACRAMENTS OF HEALING 93
PENANCE 95
From the *Catechism of the Catholic Church* 95
Rite of Penance (Form A) 96
15. Why Go to Confession? –
John F. Baldovin, SJ 99
16. How to Go to Confession –
Kurt Stasiak, OSB 103
CONVERSATION QUESTIONS 108

ANOINTING OF THE SICK.................................109
From the *Catechism of the Catholic Church* 109
Anointing of the Sick Outside of Mass...........................110
17. The Richness of Tradition –
Lizette Larson-Miller 112
18. Anointing as Pastoral Sacrament –
Bruce T. Morrill, SJ 118
CONVERSATION QUESTIONS 125

PART FOUR: SACRAMENTS OF VOCATION 127
MARRIAGE 129
From the *Catechism of the Catholic Church* 129
Nuptial Blessing (Form C) 130

Contents

19. The Sacrament of Marriage –
Michael G. Lawler and William P. Roberts 132

20. A Promised Lifetime – *Colleen Campion* 136

21. Faithful Love – *Melinda Brown Donovan* 140

CONVERSATION QUESTIONS 142

HOLY ORDERS 143

From the *Catechism of the Catholic Church* 143

Ordination Examinations 144

22. Ordained Ministry: A Brief History –
Sharon L. McMillan, SNDdeN 149

23. Presbyteral Identity within Parish Identity –
Susan K. Wood, SCL 156

CONVERSATION QUESTIONS 160

CONCLUSION 161

Sacraments: Visible Words of Friendship –
David Farina Turnbloom 163

ACKNOWLEDGMENTS 169

NOTES 173

CONTRIBUTORS 179

Preface

This book contains a collection of passages from the *Catechism of the Catholic Church*, excerpts from official rubrics of sacramental rites, chapters written by liturgical theologians, and suggested questions for discussion. All of these texts are printed here with the intention of highlighting the connections between sacramental theology and sacramental prayers.

The book is divided into four main parts. The first part, entitled "Why the Sacraments?" treats the sacraments in general, focusing on the central role they play in the Catholic faith. The remaining parts will treat the sacraments of initiation (part 2), the sacraments of healing (part 3), and the sacraments of vocation (part 4). The treatment of each sacrament begins with selected passages from the *Catechism of the Catholic Church* that offer succinct descriptions of the sacrament and its role in the life of the Church. Second is an excerpt from the prayers used in the celebration of that sacrament followed by responses by theologians with expertise in the history and theology of that sacrament. Finally, there are discussion questions so that you can examine the significance of the sacraments in your daily life.

These texts provide sources for students and teachers, for Catholics and non-Catholics, for Christians and non-Christians, and for the laity and the ordained. It is our hope that this collection of texts, reflections, and questions will assist readers in recognizing and engaging the sacraments as the heart of Christian discipleship.

John F. Baldovin, SJ, and David Farina Turnbloom

ix

PART ONE

WHY THE SACRAMENTS?

✝

FROM THE *CATECHISM OF THE CATHOLIC CHURCH*

1076 The Church was made manifest to the world on the day of Pentecost by the outpouring of the Holy Spirit.[1] The gift of the Spirit ushers in a new era in the "dispensation of the mystery"— the age of the Church, during which Christ manifests, makes present, and communicates his work of salvation through the liturgy of his Church, "until he comes" [1 Cor 11:26]. In this age of the Church Christ now lives and acts in and with his Church, in a new way appropriate to this new age. He acts through the sacraments in what the common Tradition of the East and the West calls "the sacramental economy"; this is the communication (or "dispensation") of the fruits of Christ's Paschal mystery in the celebration of the Church's "sacramental" liturgy.

1115 Jesus' words and actions during his hidden life and public ministry were already salvific, for they anticipated the power of his Paschal mystery. They announced and prepared what he was going to give the Church when all was accomplished. The mysteries of Christ's life are the foundations of what he would henceforth dispense in the sacraments, through the ministers of his Church, for "what was visible in our Savior has passed over into his mysteries."[2]

1116 Sacraments are "powers that come forth" from the Body of Christ, which is ever-living and life-giving [cf. Luke 5:17; 6:19; 8:46]. They are actions of the Holy Spirit at work in his Body, the Church. They are "the masterworks of God" in the new and everlasting covenant.

1118 The sacraments are "of the Church" in the double sense that they are "by her" and "for her." They are "by the Church," for she is the sacrament of Christ's action at work in her through the mission of the Holy Spirit. They are "for the Church" in the sense that "the sacraments make the Church,"[3] since they manifest and communicate to men, above all in the Eucharist, the mystery of communion with the God who is love, One in three persons.

GOD'S GRANDEUR

The world is charged with the grandeur of God.
  It will flame out, like shining from shook foil;
  It gathers to a greatness, like the ooze of oil
Crushed. Why do men then now not reck his rod?
Generations have trod, have trod, have trod;
  And all is seared with trade; bleared, smeared with toil;
  And wears man's smudge and shares man's smell: the soil
Is bare now, nor can foot feel, being shod.

And for all this, nature is never spent;
  There lives the dearest freshness deep down things;
And though the last lights off the black West went
  Oh, morning, at the brown brink eastward, springs—
Because the Holy Ghost over the bent
  World broods with warm breast and with ah!
    bright wings.

Gerard Manley Hopkins, SJ

1. Catholics

A Sacramental People

JOHN F. BALDOVIN, SJ

The first line of "God's Grandeur" by Gerard Manley Hopkins is a fine starting point for considering the importance of sacraments and sacramentality for Catholics. The best of our Catholic tradition has always shown an immense respect for and appreciation of the goodness of God's creation. Put simply, we don't believe that it's necessary to flee the world and created things to encounter God. On the contrary, it is because of the goodness of creation, and especially because God chose to commit himself irrevocably to humankind and our created world in the incarnation, that we believe that God encounters us through what he has made. Put another way, God doesn't communicate his life to us despite our created, physical, human condition but precisely in the midst of it.

Moreover, a number of twentieth-century Catholic theologians, especially Karl Rahner, SJ, and Edward Schillebeeckx, OP, helped us to recover the idea that in a fundamental way Christ is the sacrament of God and that the Church is the primary sacrament of Christ in the world. It's on this basis that we can understand the seven sacraments of the Church as genuine engagements with Christ through his Church. Each of the individual sacraments helps us to encounter the incarnate Lord Jesus and to enter into the effects of his saving passion, death, and resurrection in a different way. It has been said, quite correctly, that we better understand the sacraments as verbs than as nouns. In other words, they are the actions of the risen Lord transforming us more and more into his

Body. This is a fine way to appreciate our participation in Christ's returning creation back to the Father by our common participation in his priesthood. This is the Church's fundamental priesthood, which is served by the ordained priesthood. This is why baptism, which makes us a part of the common priesthood, is so important.

The *Catechism of the Catholic Church* pointedly does not take a one-size-fits-all approach to the sacraments. Instead, it presents them in three groupings. The first grouping is sacraments of initiation: baptism, confirmation, and the Eucharist. Note that this is the original sequence of Christian initiation, which has now been recovered in the Rite of Christian Initiation of Adults (RCIA). The questions raised by making confirmation into a sacrament of "Christian maturity" are raised later in this book. Of course, the supreme sacrament is the culmination and high point of Christian initiation: the Holy Eucharist, in which Christ gives himself to us in his body and blood. It is very helpful to understand the Eucharist as the ongoing sacrament of Christian initiation, in which we are helped to become more and more what we receive—Christ.

The *Catechism* goes on to treat two sacraments that heal our baptismal status when it is broken or wounded. These are the sacraments of penance and of the anointing of the sick. The experience of both of these sacraments has been significantly transformed in the wake of the liturgical reforms that followed the Second Vatican Council. Confession of sin to a priest has become rarer but perhaps more significant. Anointing of the sick is no longer "extreme unction," the sacrament of the dying, but rather a sacrament that helps the seriously ill to encounter the healing power of Christ in the midst of his community. As the chapters on these sacraments help to point out, we now understand these sacraments in the context of pastoral care. In other words, they are ideally not so much discreet moments as they are high points of a process of Christian life.

The final two sacraments are called *sacraments at the service of communion*—what we call the sacraments of vocation. Holy orders and holy matrimony, each in its own way, help to build up the Christian community by incarnating God's service to us (holy orders) and God's love for the world (marriage). Each of these sacraments is realized more in being lived out than simply in the ceremonies that initiate them.

Like the Eucharist, which I call a many-faceted jewel, all of the sacraments are many-faceted and exhibit God's grace for us in ways that defy simple, neat definitions. In other words, the sacraments realize—make real—the graced experiences of our daily lives, and by ritualizing those experiences, they nourish us with further grace in a kind of blessed circle to live our lives as members of Christ's Body, his common priesthood.

2. What Makes Us Catholic?

Thomas H. Groome

Catholic Christianity emphasizes that the divine-human covenant is enacted within everyday life; *here* is where "it's at" between ourselves and God. *Here* God reaches out and engages with us. *Here* we respond as partners. Catholic tradition gathers up this conviction that our covenant is realized through ordinary life in the principle of sacramentality. Nothing is more significant to *what makes us catholic* than the sacramental principle. It epitomizes a Catholic outlook on life in the world; if allowed only one word to describe Catholic imagination, we'd have to say *sacramental.*

Theologian Richard McBrien writes, "No theological principle or focus is more characteristic of Catholicism or more central to its identity than the principle of sacramentality." Although this is surely true, Catholic Christians tend to associate sacramentality too exclusively with what happens in church, with the celebration of the seven sacraments. The principle of sacramentality, however, reaches far beyond liturgical rites. In fact, the great sacraments are simply climactic celebrations of the sacramentality of life.

The sacramental principle means that *God is present to humankind and we respond to God's grace through ordinary and everyday life in the world.* In other words, God's Spirit and humankind work together through nature and creation, through culture and society, through our minds and bodies, hearts and souls, through our labors and efforts, creativity and generativity, in the depth of our own being and in community with others, through the events and experiences that come our way, through what we are doing and what is "going on" around us, through everything and anything of life. *Life in the world is sacramental—* the medium of God's outreach and of human response.

Saint Augustine defined a sacrament as "a visible sign of invisible grace." The sacramental principle proposes that everything in our life-world can be such a sign. In the classic phrase of Ignatius of Loyola, Christians are invited "to see God in all things." Christian faith also claims that God's saving work in Jesus has heightened the sacramentality of life. Christians believe that Jesus was the primary sacrament of God to the world; empowered by the Spirit, Jesus was God's saving presence as one of us. What could be more "ordinary" than that? And the Spirit continues the sacramental effect of Jesus throughout human history.

Understood within the sacramentality of life in the world, the seven sacraments are sacred symbols that mediate God's grace in Jesus with heightened effect. They do this by the power of the Holy Spirit working through the Christian community. Each sacrament is a way of encountering the risen Christ and of receiving the particular grace that the sacrament symbolizes, whether initiating, empowering, sustaining, forgiving, healing, serving, or bonding. But Catholic Christians should never think of the seven sacraments as apart from life. All must be appreciated as apex moments that heighten and celebrate the sacramentality of life in the world.

Note that all the sacraments are symbolized by the "ordinary" of life, by bread, wine, water, oil, touch, words, gestures, and lovemaking in marriage. Each symbolizes something profoundly everyday that by the power of God's Spirit continues the saving mission of Jesus, enacting a climactic moment in the divine-human partnership. As theologian Rosemary Haughton writes, "Sacraments are extraordinary experiences of the ordinary."

CATHOLIC SACRAMENTS

Baptism symbolizes all human experiences of partnership and community, of belonging and vocation, as it initiates people into the Body of Christ—the Church—to live as disciples of Jesus toward the reign of God.

Confirmation symbolizes the human *spirit* of faith, hope, and love, and continues to initiate into Christian community by "sealing" Christians with the gifts of the Holy Spirit, strengthening them to live their faith in the world.

Eucharist symbolizes all that reflects vitality and responsibility, peace and justice, care and compassion—everything that fulfills the covenant—as it celebrates the *real* presence of the risen Christ, makes "an offering of praise" to God, bonds Christians into community, sustains them with the "bread of life," and empowers them "for the life of the world" (John 6:51). Eucharist is "the Sacrament of sacraments" (*Catechism*, 1330) and for Christian faith the most eminent instance of divine-human encounter.

Reconciliation symbolizes all human efforts at forgiveness, peacemaking, and clemency as it celebrates God's never-ending mercy for repentant sinners, mediated through a Christian community.

Anointing of the sick symbolizes all human efforts at healing the ill, sustaining the elderly, and consoling the dying as it celebrates and mediates God's power to restore people to health—spiritual, physical, and psychological—or to give hope for eternal life.

Holy orders symbolizes the vocation that everyone has to worthwhile work; it officially ordains a person to function as a leader in the Christian community's ministries of preaching, celebrating sacraments, and enabling the gifts of all to work well together with "holy order."

Matrimony symbolizes all experiences of friendship and support, all of human intimacy and sexuality, as it celebrates the covenant of life and love between a married couple.

In traditional Catholic theology, the effectiveness of a sacrament depends both on the action of the Spirit and on the response of the person and community celebrating it—as always, a covenant. There is nothing magical about sacraments. True, they mediate God's grace, but they also bring the "response-ability" to live as graced people. For example, Eucharist enables people to encounter the real presence of the risen Christ, and it sends them to "love and serve" after the way of Jesus.

Similarly, for the sacramentality of life in general, God's grace works through the ordinary and everyday but also expects our partnership and responsibility. Though enabled by God's Spirit, we must make our own good choices and best efforts.

Therefore, Catholicism invites people to adopt a sacramental outlook on all of life in the world. In the words of the poet Gerard Manley Hopkins (1844–89): "The world is charged with the grandeur of God! It will flame out, like shining from shook foil." That's a Catholic imagination!

CONVERSATION QUESTIONS

1. It was noted that "we don't believe that it's necessary to flee the world and created things to encounter God." Where do you most often encounter God in your daily life?

2. To which sacraments do you feel most connected? How have those sacraments played an important role in your life? From which sacraments do you feel most disconnected? How do you think you might foster a deeper connection to those sacraments?

3. What are the times in your daily life that most relate to your experiences of the sacraments (e.g. playing, cooking, teaching, etc.)? How can you be more attentive to God's presence in such events?

4. How might you develop your own sacramental consciousness, being more alert for God/grace moments in daily life?

PART TWO

SACRAMENTS
OF INITIATION

✝

FROM THE *CATECHISM OF THE CATHOLIC CHURCH*

1212 The sacraments of Christian initiation—Baptism, Confirmation, and the Eucharist—lay the *foundations* of every Christian life. "The sharing in the divine nature given to men through the grace of Christ bears a certain likeness to the origin, development, and nourishing of natural life. The faithful are born anew by Baptism, strengthened by the sacrament of Confirmation, and receive in the Eucharist the food of eternal life. By means of these sacraments of Christian initiation, they thus receive in increasing measure the treasures of the divine life and advance toward the perfection of charity."[1]

1229 From the time of the apostles, becoming a Christian has been accomplished by a journey and initiation in several stages. This journey can be covered rapidly or slowly, but certain essential elements will always have to be present: proclamation of the word, acceptance of the Gospel entailing conversion, profession of faith, Baptism itself, the outpouring of the Holy Spirit, and admission to Eucharistic communion.

3. A Rite of Passage

AIDAN J. KAVANAGH, OSB

I have always rather liked the gruff robustness of the first rubric for baptism found in a late fourth-century church order that directs the bishop to enter the vestibule of the baptistery and say to the candidates, without commentary or apology, only four words: "Take off your clothes." There is no evidence that the assistants fainted or the candidates asked what he meant.

Teaching and much prayer and fasting had led them to understand that the language of their passage this night in Christ from death to life would be the language of the bathhouse and the tomb.

So they stripped and stood there, probably faint from fasting, shivering from the cold of early Easter morning, and in awe at what was about to transpire. Years of formation were about to be consummated; years of having their motives and lives scrutinized; years of hearing the word of God read; years of being dismissed with prayer before the faithful went on to celebrate the Eucharist; years of seeing the tomblike baptistery building only from the outside; years of hearing the old folks of the community tell hair-raising tales of what being a Christian had cost their own grandparents when the emperors were still pagan; years of a vagueness concerning what was actually done by the faithful at the breaking of bread and in that closed baptistery.

Tonight, all this was about to end as they stood naked on a cold floor in the gloom of this eerie room.

Abruptly, the bishop demands that they face westward, toward where the sun dies, swallowed up in darkness, and denounce the king of shadows and death and "things that go bump in the night." Each one of them comes forward to do this loudly under the hooded gaze of the bishop (who is tired from presiding all night at the vigil continuing next door in the church); deacons shield the nudity of the male candidates from the women, and deaconesses screen the women in the same manner. This is when they finally surrender the world and life as they have known it; the umbilical cord is cut, but they have not yet begun to breathe.

Then they must each turn eastward toward where the sun surges up bathed in a light, which just now can be seen stealing into the windows of the room. They must voice their acceptance of the King of light and life, who has trampled down death by his own death. As each one finishes this, he or she is fallen upon by a deacon or a deaconess who vigorously rubs olive oil into his or her body, as the bishop perhaps dozes off briefly, leaning on his cane. (He is like an old surgeon waiting for the operation to begin.)

When all the candidates have been thoroughly oiled, they and the bishop are suddenly startled by the crash of the baptistery doors being thrown open. Brilliant golden light spills out into the shadowy vestibule, and following the bishop (who has now regained his composure), the candidates and the assistant priests, deacons, deaconesses, and sponsors move into the most glorious room most of them have ever seen. It is a high, arbor-like pavilion of green, gold, purple, and white mosaic from marble floor to domed ceiling sparkling like jewels in the light of innumerable oil lamps that fill the room with heady warmth. The windows are beginning to blaze with the light of Easter dawn....And above all these, in the highest point of the ballooning dome, a giant icon of a naked Jesus (very much in the flesh) stands up to his waist in the Jordan as an unkempt John pours water on him and God's disembodied hand points the Holy Spirit at Jesus' head in the form of a white bird.

Suddenly, the candidates realize that they have unconsciously formed themselves into a mirror image of this icon of Jesus. They are standing around a pool...into which gushes water pouring noisily from the mouth of a stone lion crouching atop a pillar at poolside. The bishop stands beside this, his priests on each side; a deacon has entered the pool, and the other assistants are trying to maintain a modicum of decorum among the candidates who forget their nakedness as they crowd close to see. The room is warm, humid, and it glows. It is a golden paradise in a bathhouse in a mausoleum, an oasis, Eden restored: the navel of the world, where death and life meet...and become indistinguishable from each other.

The bishop rumbles a massive prayer—something about the Spirit and the waters of life and death—and then pokes the water a few times with his cane. The candidates recall Moses doing something like that to a rock from which water flowed, and they are mightily impressed. Then a young male candidate of about ten, the son of pious parents, is led down into the pool by the deacon. The water is warm (it has been heated in a furnace), and the oil on his body spreads out on the surface in iridescent swirls. The deacon positions the child near the cascade from the lion's mouth. The bishop leans over on his cane, and in a voice that sounds like something out of the Apocalypse, says: "Euphemius! Do you believe in God the Father, who created all of heaven and earth?" After a nudge from the deacon beside him, the boy murmurs that he does. And just in time, for the deacon, who has been doing this for fifty years and is the boy's grandfather, wraps him in his arms, lifts him backward into the rushing water, and forces him under the surface. The old deacon smiles through his beard at the wide brown eyes that look up at him in shock and fear from beneath the water (the boy has purposely not been told what to expect).

Then he raises him up coughing and sputtering. The bishop waits until he can speak again, and leaning over a second time, tapping the boy on the shoulder with his cane, says: "Euphemius!

18

Do you believe in Jesus Christ, God's only Son, who was conceived of the Virgin Mary, suffered under Pontius Pilate, and was crucified, died, and was buried? Who rose on the third day and ascended into heaven, from whence he will come again to judge the living and the dead?" This time he replies like a shot, "I do," and then holds his nose...down he goes. "Euphemius! Do you believe in the Holy Spirit, the master and giver of life, who proceeds from the Father, who is to be honored and glorified equally with the Father and the Son, who spoke by the prophets? And in one holy, catholic, and apostolic Church which is the communion of God's holy ones? And in the life that is coming?" "I do."

When he comes up the third time, his grandfather gathers him in his vast arms and carries him up the steps leading out of the pool. There another deacon roughly dries Euphemius with a warm towel, and a senior priest, who is almost ninety and is regarded by all as a "confessor" because he was imprisoned for the faith as a young man, tremulously pours perfumed oil from a glass pitcher over the boy's damp head until it soaks his hair and runs down over his upper body. The fragrance of this enormously expensive oil fills the room as the old man mutters, "God's servant, Euphemius, is anointed in the name of the Father, Son, and Holy Spirit." Euphemius is then wrapped in a new linen tunic; the fragrant chrism seeps into it, and he is given a burning terracotta oil lamp and told to go stand by the door and keep quiet. Meanwhile, the other baptisms have continued.

When all have been done in this same manner (an old deaconess, a widow, replaced Euphemius's grandfather when it came the women's time), the clergy strike up the Easter hymn, "Christ is risen from the dead, he has crushed death by his death and bestowed life on those who lay in the tomb."

The whole baptismal party—tired, damp, thrilled, and oily—walk out into the blaze of Easter morning and, led by the bishop, go next door to the church. There the bishop bangs on the closed doors with his cane; they are flung open, the endless vigil is halted, and the baptismal party enters as all take up the hymn "Christ is risen," which is all but drowned out by the ovations that greet Christ truly risen in his newly born ones. As they enter, the fragrance of chrism fills the church; it is the Easter smell. The pious struggle to get near the newly baptized in order to touch their chrismed hair and rub its fragrance on their own faces. All is chaos until the baptismal party manages to reach the towering ambo that stands in the middle of the pewless hall. The bishop ascends its lower front steps, turns to face the white-clad neophytes, the newly baptized, grouped at the bottom with their burning lamps, and the boisterous faithful now held back by a group of well-built acolytes and doorkeepers. Euphemius's mother has fainted and been carried outside for some air.

The bishop opens his arms to the neophytes and once again all burst into "Christ is risen," *Christos aneste*. He then affirms and seals their baptism after prayer, for all the faithful to see, with an authoritative gesture—laying his hand on each head, signing each oily forehead once again in the form of a cross, while booming out, "The servant of God is sealed with the Holy Spirit." To which all reply a thunderous "Amen." And for the first time the former candidates receive and give the kiss of peace. Everyone is in tears. While this continues, bread and wine are laid out on the holy table; the bishop then prays at great length over them after things quiet down, and the neophytes lead all to communion with Euphemius out in front.

While his grandfather holds his lamp, Euphemius dines on the precious body whose true and undoubted member he has become; he drinks the precious Blood of him in whom he himself has now died; and just this once he drinks from two other special cups—one containing baptismal water, the other containing milk and honey mixed as a gustatory icon of the promised land into which he and his colleagues have finally entered out of the desert through Jordan's waters. Then his mother (now recovered and somewhat pale, still insisting she had only stumbled) takes him home and puts him, fragrantly, to bed.

Euphemius has come a long way. He has passed from death into a life he lives still, in eternity.

CONVERSATION QUESTIONS

1. What is most striking in the above passage about the way ancient Christians celebrated initiation? Are there aspects of these ancient practices that you would like to see happen today? Are there aspects that you are happy to leave behind?

2. The passage above describes all three sacraments being celebrated together. Do you think there are advantages in celebrating all three sacraments together? Are there advantages in spacing them out over the course of childhood and adolescence?

3. What does it mean to die with Christ? What does it mean to be reborn with Christ?

4. What do you recognize as the daily demands of your own baptism? How can you respond more faithfully?

BAPTISM

†

1239 The *essential rite* of the sacrament follows: *Baptism* properly speaking. It signifies and actually brings about death to sin and entry into the life of the Most Holy Trinity through configuration to the Paschal mystery of Christ. Baptism is performed in the most expressive way by triple immersion in the baptismal water. However, from ancient times it has also been able to be conferred by pouring the water three times over the candidate's head.

1213 Holy Baptism is the basis of the whole Christian life, the gateway to life in the Spirit (*vitae spiritualis ianua*),[1] and the door which gives access to the other sacraments. Through Baptism we are freed from sin and reborn as sons of God; we become members of Christ, are incorporated into the Church and made sharers in her mission: "Baptism is the sacrament of regeneration through water in the word."[2]

1267 Baptism makes us members of the Body of Christ: "Therefore…we are members one of another" [Eph 4:25]. Baptism incorporates us *into the Church*. From the baptismal fonts is born the one People of God of the New Covenant, which transcends all the natural or human limits of nations, cultures, races, and sexes: "For by one Spirit we were all baptized into one body" [1 Cor 12:13].

1268 The baptized have become "living stones" to be "built into a spiritual house, to be a holy priesthood" [1 Pet 2:5]. By Baptism they share in the priesthood of Christ, in his prophetic and royal mission. They are "a chosen race, a royal priesthood, a holy nation, God's own people, that [they] may declare the wonderful deeds of him who called [them] out of darkness into his marvelous light" [1 Pet 2:9]. *Baptism gives a share in the common priesthood of all believers.*

BLESSING AND INVOCATION OF GOD OVER BAPTISMAL WATER (FORM A)

My dear brothers and sisters, God uses the sacrament of water to give his divine life to those who believe in him. Let us turn to him, and ask him to pour his gift of life from this font on this child he has chosen.

Then, turning to the font, he says the following blessing:

O God, who by invisible power
accomplish a wondrous effect
through sacramental signs
and who in many ways have prepared water, your
    creation,
to show forth the grace of Baptism;

O God, whose Spirit
in the first moments of the world's creation
hovered over the waters,
so that the very substance of water
would even then take to itself the power to sanctify;

O God, who by the outpouring of the flood
foreshadowed regeneration,
so that from the mystery of one and the same element
    of water
would come an end to vice and a beginning of virtue;

O God, who caused the children of Abraham
to pass dry-shod through the Red Sea,
so that the chosen people,
set free from slavery to Pharaoh,
would prefigure the people of the baptized;

O God, whose Son,
baptized by John in the waters of the Jordan,
was anointed with the Holy Spirit,
and, as he hung upon the Cross,
gave forth water from his side along with blood,
and after his Resurrection, commanded his disciples:
"Go forth, teach all nations, baptizing them
in the name of the Father and of the Son and of the Holy
    Spirit,"

look now, we pray, upon the face of your Church
and graciously unseal for her the fountain of Baptism.
May this water receive by the Holy Spirit
the grace of your Only Begotten Son,
so that human nature, created in your image
and washed clean through the Sacrament of Baptism
from all the squalor of the life of old,
may be found worthy to rise to the life of newborn
    children
through water and the Holy Spirit.

CATHOLIC SACRAMENTS

The celebrant touches the water with his right hand and continues:

May the power of the Holy Spirit,
O Lord, we pray,
come down through your Son
into the fullness of this font,
so that all who have been buried with Christ
by Baptism into death
may rise again to life with him.
Who lives and reigns with you in the unity of the
     Holy Spirit,
one God, for ever and ever.

4. Baptizing a Child

MARY ANN CLARAHAN

In structure, the Rite of Baptism of a child is set up like a stational liturgy, with processions to different stations: from the church door, to ambo, to font, to altar. Each place is a point of encounter with Christ, who greets, speaks his word, and baptizes. If circumstances allow, some or all those present can follow in procession from station to station, accompanied by appropriate music. If there is no choir, songs already in the parish repertoire may be chosen. Coordinating these elements takes time and effort and is open to adaptation.

THE FIRST STATION: THE CHURCH DOOR

The rite suggests that "reception of the child/children" begins at the church door where the celebrant greets those to be baptized with their parents and godparents (nos. 32–42). It is here that the parents are questioned and publicly declare their faith, the faith of the Church that they want to share with their child. The nature of this dialogue speaks of the solemnity and seriousness of the commitment the parents and Christian community are making. Not only should the following question by the celebrant be heard, but also the parents' response to it: "What do you ask of God's Church for your child?" The suggested variety of responses—baptism, faith, the grace of Christ, entrance into the

Church, eternal life—reveals the many meanings of baptism that will emerge.

Why does the Church ask the second question, "What name do you give your child?" A name gives flesh to the value that we have for children. He or she is a person—not a number—a person in relationship to God, family, and church community. He or she is a gift. A name also sets one out on a mission. Such an understanding stands in opposition to a world that speaks of a baby in terms of "tissue" and a sex-trade economy that views children as commodities to be sold. Therefore, considering the significance of a name to the child, to the parents, and to the Church, even if several children are being baptized, it is worth considering the value of allowing one parent of each child to speak that name. A personal example occurred when my sister's third of six children was baptized. There were five other babies being christened that day. Unfortunately, the priest approached the celebration with a rather minimalist view. When it came time to respond to "What name do you give this child?" he asked the parents to respond all together. No name was clearly heard. I saw my sister's eyes glaze over. After the celebration, she told me how disappointed she was at not being able to speak her child's name for all to hear. Her next three children were baptized in another parish, with a more ritually sensitive celebrant. This applies to the question posed to the godparents as well. Their oral response makes a difference.

This initial part of the baptismal rite ends with the celebrant's words addressed to the child, affirming the child's dignity and identity in relationship to Christ and the Christian community. He says:

> The Christian community welcomes you with great joy. In its name I claim you for Christ our Savior by the sign of his cross. (no. 41)

Claimed for Christ with the distinguishing sign of crucified and risen love, the celebrant, each parent, and the godparents trace the sign of the cross on the child's forehead, in silence. So powerful is this gesture that added words, music, or commentary would overshadow and minimize this palpable mediation of faith. As part of a reflection for parents after their child's baptism, it would be interesting to ask them: What did this signing mean to you? What did you feel toward your child as you did this?

THE SECOND STATION: THE AMBO

The celebrant then invites the parents, godparents, and all assembled to move to the second station for the Liturgy of the Word. Why not proclaim the Liturgy of the Word at the ambo? Celebration at this symbolic place, which is used for the proclamation of the word at Sunday Eucharist, highlights the presence of God in both Word and Sacrament, and the connection between baptism and Eucharist. As in every liturgical celebration, members of the assembly should be called upon to proclaim the word and announce the bidding prayers (intercessions), perhaps someone from the family. These roles can be assigned in the days before the actual baptism.

The suggested biblical passages for this rite from both Hebrew and Christian Scriptures portray in story and image the Church's rich theology of baptism. In the homily it is the celebrant's task to connect these biblical narratives of salvation with God's saving work present today in this child's life and family. Cyril of Jerusalem, in his baptismal preaching, didn't rely on dogmatic statements but used a cascade of images that bombarded the imagination and appealed to the assembly's self-understanding as Christians.

Intercessions, or bidding prayers, within this rite remind the members of the assembly once again of their responsibility to pray for the newly baptized, their parents, godparents, and themselves. The litany of saints that concludes the Liturgy of the Word appeals to the full communion of saints to intercede for the baptized. The rite suggests that names of other saints such as the patrons of the children and local saints be included. What about the patron saints of deceased relatives, such as grandparents, as well?

The Rite of Baptism then moves to the prayer of exorcism and anointing before baptism. Both Prayers A and B ask God to cast out the power of Satan and free the child from original sin. This prayer of exorcism is accompanied by an anointing, asking God to strengthen the child with God's power.

In our present world climate, this child may encounter the power of evil in acts of terrorism, church scandals, government and business corruption, exploitation of the most vulnerable, and in more subtle ways as well. More catechesis is probably needed to explain the notion of *exorcism* and the power of Christ's kingdom of love within. We might ask, How does this exorcism and anointing affect the Christian's everyday living and choices?

THE THIRD STATION: THE FONT

Those to be baptized, accompanied by their parents and godparents, now move to the font. What a profusion of symbolism occurs here—from the blessing of water to the *ephphatha*, the prayers over ears and mouth! Each ritual unit holds in tension a strategic configuration of word, gesture, symbol, place, persons, movement, and silence. Allow each of these symbols to speak and to interact with one another, not just the spoken word of the prayer text. Highlighted here are only a few elements of this part of the baptismal rite.

The rich symbol of water flows through text, font, gesture, and scriptural image. In the initial invitation the celebrant reminds those gathered that through water and the Holy Spirit,

God will give this "child new life in abundance" (no. 53A). The blessing prayer over the baptismal water recalls the mystery of God's unseen power sacramentally revealed through water. In order to understand the paschal paradox of this blessing prayer, we need to acknowledge water's life-giving and death-dealing power. The water over which the Spirit breathed at the dawn of creation is also the water of the great flood; the separated waters that opened the path of freedom for the Israelites and dealt death to the Egyptians, and the water that flowed from the side of Christ, symbolizing the birth of the Church, mingled with the blood of crucifixion. In our world the water that provides refreshment and food for tourists and fishermen may later rage as a devastating tsunami, and the waters of the Mississippi Gulf, which generated jazz and economic livelihood, can submerge a whole city and take untold lives. The paschal mystery into which this child will be immersed through these baptismal waters cannot escape sharing in Christ's suffering, death, and resurrection. However, the promise of abundant life flowing from death on a cross can surmount both human sinfulness and suffering through rebirth by water and the Holy Spirit. For this reason there is need for a strong ritual action of threefold immersion or abundant pouring of water upon the child with the words, "I baptize you in the name of the Father...and of the Son...and of the Holy Spirit." Sparse drops of water don't do justice to the child's paschal immersion in trinitarian love. If possible, the child's other siblings can also surround the font as witnesses.

In the explanatory rites after baptism—anointing, clothing with a white garment, and bestowing of the lighted candle—the graced identity of this child continues to unfold in word and ritual action. The newly baptized is (1) freed from sin; (2) anointed by God as a member of Christ who is priest, prophet, and king; (3) incorporated into Christ's paschal mystery; (4) enlightened by Christ; (5) clothed in Christ; (6) a new creation; (7) an adopted child of God; (8) reborn in water and the Holy Spirit; (9) heir of eternal life; and (10) member of the Church. Each of these rites is a mediator of Christian identity and relationships. In addition, they charge the parents, godparents, and Christian community to tend to the faith of these children through word and example, so that they may "keep the flame of faith alive in their heart" (no. 64).

THE FOURTH STATION: THE ALTAR

Accompanied by lighted candles and song, the rite moves to the altar, unless the baptism was performed in the sanctuary. Moving to the altar prefigures the future sharing at the eucharistic table. The celebrant invites all to pray the Lord's Prayer. At the end there is the blessing of the mother(s), father(s), and finally of the whole assembly. When I talked to a few parents after their children's baptism, all agreed that this blessing is both touching and sobering. As they held their child in their arms, they said that a mixture of fear, joy, awe, and gratitude came over them as they were singled out for God's blessing. They also spoke of being overwhelmed at the great responsibility to bear witness to this faith for their children. Make the most out of this blessing ritually!

Finally, the whole assembly is sent out in blessing, commissioned to walk by the light of faith. Those who gathered ritually to celebrate the baptism of a child return to the door through which they entered, but it is to be hoped not unchanged. Celebrations done well with adequate sacramental catechesis hold graced possibilities of conversion and transformation for all involved.

5. Infant Baptism and Adult Faith

Michael Drumm

Baptism is a communal rather than an individual affair. No effort should be spared in doing away with any semblance of private baptism. It should never be a private family affair, and if it is, then this should be changed. A gathering of two families from hither and thither does not constitute a gathering of the *ekklesia*. The underlying reason for the "privatization" of baptism is that it is perceived in the popular mind as essentially concerned with freeing the individual from original sin while often forgetting the other central effects of the sacrament: participation in the paschal mystery, entry into the community of the Church, and the giving of the Holy Spirit.

By right, baptismal celebrations should take place during the key gathering of the local community at its Sunday Eucharist. This is not nearly as difficult as some priests suggest. It is hardly surprising that our Sunday gatherings are so anonymous when we don't even celebrate and acknowledge new members in our communities, something that most people would love to do. Of course, if a true communal emphasis is to be introduced, then the present "supermarket" syndrome of shopping around for a suitable priest and/or church must be overcome. Nothing could be more indicative of a privatized notion of baptism, which people perceive as available on demand. Given the present model for celebrating the sacrament, it is not surprising that priests who are family members or friends agree to act as celebrant even though this further corrodes the local community dynamic. Serious efforts must be made to overcome these gross misunderstandings of the sacrament, which are common among our people, including some priests. There is no pastoral or theological reason why baptism should occur in any context other than a gathering of the local parish community. It is lamentable that in our present situation the blessing of throats occasions a greater gathering of the community than baptism.

FAITH

Baptism can take place only in the context of faith. The faith referred to in infant baptism is that of the parents. One could certainly argue that only the children of those who practice should be baptized; this would be a very strict criterion, but it is definitely a coherent one. Alternatively, one might introduce a catechumenate for parents, admittedly a rather strange idea, but strange situations call for strange remedies and nothing could be stranger than baptizing the children of nonbelievers. The function of this catechumenate would be to enable parents to renew their own baptismal promises in a meaningful way so that they could sensibly promise to raise their child in the faith.

A more radical approach would actively discourage some baptisms if they amounted only to a formality undergone to satisfy cultural mores or the grandparents. One could also encourage those who sincerely doubt the sense of baptizing infants to postpone the celebration until a later time. To facilitate practices such as these, it would be helpful to introduce a rite of welcome for such infants (along the lines of the rite of becoming catechumens in the RCIA) so as to emphasize that though not baptized they are linked to the community of the church. The parish community must take responsibility for those it baptizes. It is not satisfactory to baptize and then hope that someone else will catechize. Much of our thought and energy must now be devoted to catechizing those we so readily sacramentalize.

EVANGELIZE

To preach the good news of the death and resurrection of the Lord is the origin and goal of all sacraments, especially baptism. Lent and Easter emerged as liturgical seasons to prepare for and celebrate baptism. The baptismal liturgies of Lent make little sense to our people because Lent is seen as a time of personal penitential renewal. Valid as abstaining from foods, cigarettes, and alcohol might be, it is hardly the most potent manner of reminding people of the paschal significance of their baptism. We need to retrieve Lent, Easter, and baptism from the clutches of an all-too-private piety, and that is precisely what the RCIA attempts to do. To give a proper focus to the paschal character of baptism, some suggest that we should baptize only at the Easter vigil. Again, this sounds extreme, but it has strong roots. The least one must insist upon is that baptism occur only on occasions of paschal significance, that is, on Sundays. There is no reason why it should not be limited to some Sundays of particular significance, obviously Easter and Pentecost, the other Sundays of the Easter season, Ascension and Corpus Christi, while Epiphany and the Baptism of Our Lord also suggest themselves as possibilities. Why tie baptism to certain Sundays and major feast days? That is the only way one can seriously link evangelization with sacrament; the very act of explaining why it occurs only on certain occasions would be part of the process of evangelization.

People may raise objections: it's not possible in terms of numbers; what about those who want their child baptized immediately? To the former, my reply is that it is possible; a large number of parishes have fewer than twenty baptisms a year, some have as few as half a dozen, and none has so many as to rule out a proper communal, paschal-linked celebration. At any rate, the numbers are going to become smaller and smaller. To the latter, my reply is that baptism is not an emergency rite except in an emergency. Nothing so distorts the practice of baptism than the *quam primum* idea that baptism is an emergency intervention to save the child from the wrath of God in case he or she dies; evangelization is surely required to liberate people from seriously deficient images of God, Church, and sacrament.

Postponing baptism for a short period until an occasion of key paschal significance arises provides just such an opportunity for evangelization.

If we want the sacraments to be moments of evangelization, we must allow the symbols to speak, which means overcoming our terribly minimalist approach to water, oil, bread, touch, and so on. The overflowing and abundant waters of baptism are reduced to the barest few drops from a jug; oil is used, but with great reserve. In celebrating the most gracious self-giving, we should surely be lavish in our expression.

CONVERSATION QUESTIONS

1. There are many ways to experience baptism: as the baptized, as a parent, as a godparent, as a family member, as a parish member, and more. Thinking of the baptisms you have experienced, what are the most important memories you have? What can you learn from them?

2. The *Catechism* says that by our baptism each Christian shares in the priestly, prophetic, and ruling mission of Christ. How can we live these missions in our everyday lives?

3. What does it mean to be "members of one another"? What are some demands of this membership for your everyday life?

4. Do you agree that baptism should take place during a Mass in front of the parish community? Thinking of your own parish, what effects might communal celebrations of baptism have on your community?

5. How might these reflections renew your commitment to living your own baptism?

CONFIRMATION

†

FROM THE *CATECHISM*
OF THE *CATHOLIC CHURCH*

1302 It is evident from its celebration that the effect of the sacrament of Confirmation is the full outpouring of the Holy Spirit as once granted to the apostles on the day of Pentecost.

1303 From this fact, Confirmation brings an increase and deepening of baptismal grace:

- it roots us more deeply in the divine filiation which makes us cry, "Abba! Father!" [Rom 8:15];

- it unites us more firmly to Christ;

- it increases the gifts of the Holy Spirit in us;

- it renders our bond with the Church more perfect;[1]

- it gives us a special strength of the Holy Spirit to spread and defend the faith by word and action as true witnesses of Christ, to confess the name of Christ boldly, and never to be ashamed of the Cross:[2]

Recall then that you have received the spiritual seal, the spirit of wisdom and understanding, the spirit of right judgment and courage, the spirit of knowledge and reverence, the spirit of holy fear in God's presence. Guard what you have received. God the Father has marked you with his sign; Christ the Lord has confirmed you and has placed his pledge, the Spirit, in your hearts.[3]

RITE OF CONFIRMATION WITHIN MASS

THE LAYING ON OF HANDS

The concelebrating priests stand near the bishop. He faces the people and with hands joined, sings or says:

My dear friends:
in Baptism God our Father gave the new birth of
        eternal life
to his chosen sons and daughters.
Let us pray to our Father
that he will pour out the Holy Spirit
to strengthen his sons and daughters with his gifts
and anoint them to be more like Christ the Son of God.

All pray in silence for a short time.
The bishop and the priests who will minister the sacrament with him lay hands upon all the candidates (by extending their hands over them). The bishop alone sings or says:

All-powerful God,
Father of our Lord Jesus Christ,
by water and the Holy Spirit
you freed your sons and daughters from sin

and gave them new life.
Send your Holy Spirit upon them
to be their helper and guide.

Give them the spirit of wisdom and understanding,
the spirit of right judgment and courage,
the spirit of knowledge and reverence.
Fill them with the spirit of wonder and awe
in your presence.
We ask this through Christ our Lord.

R. **Amen**

THE ANOINTING WITH CHRISM

The deacon brings the chrism to the bishop. Each candidate goes to the bishop, or the bishop may go to the individual candidates. The one who presented the candidate places his (her) right hand on the latter's shoulder and gives the candidate's name to the bishop; or the candidate may give his (her) own name.

The bishop dips his right thumb in the chrism and makes the sign of the cross on the forehead of the one to be confirmed, as he says:

N. Be sealed with the gift of the Holy Spirit.

The newly confirmed responds:

R. **Amen.**

The bishop says:

N. Peace be with you.

The newly confirmed responds:

R. **And with your spirit.**

6. The Missionary Nature of Confirmation

MARC B. CARON

"You will receive power when the Holy Spirit has come upon you; and you will be my witnesses." This passage from Acts 1:8 was the theme of World Youth Day 2008 in Sydney, Australia.

The theme evoked both the name that the Portuguese explorer Pedro Fernandez de Quiros gave to the continent in 1606—the Southern Land of the Holy Spirit—and the sacrament of confirmation.

During that World Youth Day, Pope Benedict XVI confirmed twenty-four young people (fourteen Australians and ten from other continents) at a Mass in which 400,000 pilgrims participated. During the Liturgy of the Eucharist, the relationship of confirmation and Eucharist was stressed as the pope distributed communion to the *confirmandi*.

Long before that communion rite at the Mass at Randwick Racecourse, the connection between the sacraments of initiation was clearly demonstrated to the participants. Their several-mile walk the day before the Mass took them over the Sydney Harbour Bridge. As they journeyed on that iconic bridge, the texts in the pilgrim's guide called attention to the new life that the sacrament of baptism brings. After recalling water's role in the history of salvation, the text stated:

The water that flows beneath our feet recalls for us the gifts that we have received in Baptism and which we renew today....Lord, we want to renew our Baptismal promises and our rejection of sin, so that we may live in freedom as your children. Pour your Holy Spirit upon us, so that we may receive the strength and courage we need to live according to the faith we profess. (World Youth Day Liturgy 2008, Liturgy Guide, 66)

From the start of World Youth Day 2008 on July 15, the *confirmandi*, along with all of the pilgrims, were being prepared for the celebration of the sacrament of confirmation during the closing Mass with Pope Benedict XVI and four hundred other bishops.

As the pilgrims approached Randwick Racecourse the day before the closing Mass, they stopped at seven specially designated "power stations" along the way. Each of these stations corresponded to a gift of the Holy Spirit. Pilgrims reflected on each gift at each location. That evening, during the prayer vigil at which Pope Benedict XVI presided, seven young pilgrims offered their personal testimony about the gifts of the Holy Spirit. The holy father responded with an address that touched upon Saint Augustine's teaching on the nature and action of the Holy Spirit in the life of the baptized. When the twenty-four candidates for confirmation were presented to the holy father, he prayed an originally composed text, invoking the Holy Spirit upon the candidates and on all gathered with him that night.

Sunday morning began with the celebration of Morning Prayer for the pilgrims with texts borrowed from the Liturgy of the Hours for Pentecost Sunday. Texts for Mass on Sunday morning were taken from the ritual Masses for Confirmation (Ritual Masses #4 A and B, Preface 54). The scripture readings obviously evoked the day of Pentecost (Acts 2:1–11), the diversity of gifts the

Spirit provides (1 Cor 12:4—13), and Jesus' mission to the world under the impulse of the Holy Spirit (Luke 4:16–22a). The Rite of Confirmation followed the usual order: the call of the candidates, the homily, renewal of baptismal promises, the laying on hands, the anointing with chrism, and general intercessions.

Overall, the celebration of confirmation during World Youth Day 2008 in Sydney was placed consistently in a missionary context. This missionary mandate from Christ is exactly what the pilgrims and the newly confirmed shared.

Theologians continue to point out that there are many ways to describe the effects of the Holy Spirit through the sacrament of confirmation. The *Catechism of the Catholic Church* refers to confirmation completing baptismal grace, binding the baptized more perfectly to the Church, and enriching them with a special strength of the Holy Spirit (1285). The increase and deepening of baptismal grace in confirmation roots us more firmly in our relationship with God the Father, unites us more closely to Christ, increases the gifts of the Holy Spirit in us, and perfects our bond with the Church (1303). The *Catechism* goes on to state that confirmation "gives us a special strength of the Holy Spirit to spread and defend the faith by word and action as true witnesses of Christ, to confess the name of Christ boldly, and never to be ashamed of the Cross" (1303).

This "power to profess faith in Christ publicly" (1305), has been most clearly associated with the teaching of Saint Thomas Aquinas on confirmation (*STh* III, 72, 5, ad. 2). It is this latter point that the various celebrations of World Youth Day highlighted. This power to profess faith publicly was implicit in the theme for this event in Sydney: "You will receive power when the Holy Spirit has come upon you; and you will be my witnesses." It is perhaps the aspect of confirmation that is most readily applicable to those baptized Roman Catholics, like the World Youth Day pilgrims, who have already been receiving communion for some years, and who now complete the grace of their baptism through the reception of the sacrament of confirmation. It is also the aspect of confirmation that organizers wanted all the pilgrims to take home with them. In a world much in need of the good news of Christ, the young pilgrims of Sydney were reminded of their responsibility to transform the world more and more into the likeness of the kingdom of God.

7. Anointed to Proclaim the Kingdom

LIAM BERGIN

Debates continue about how and when the sacrament of confirmation should be celebrated. Whatever position one takes, there is general agreement that in this sacrament the Spirit is given. In fact, the *Catechism of the Catholic Church* tells us that confirmation is the full outpouring of the Holy Spirit as once granted to the apostles on the day of Pentecost (1302). It then goes on to list how confirmation brings an "increase and deepening of Baptismal grace" (1303).

Dominican theologian Yves Congar notes that from the moment of his conception in the womb of the Virgin Mary, Jesus bore the gift of the Holy Spirit.[1] Later, at his baptism in the Jordan, the Spirit descended again to identify him as the beloved Son of God who would bring salvation to the nations. Congar argues that in the incarnation of Jesus we find the origins of Christian baptism, through which the Spirit of God gives life. Then, he claims, in the baptism of Jesus in the Jordan we find the origins of the sacrament of confirmation, in which the Spirit of God is given to proclaim the kingdom of God. That's the sequence we see in the Synoptic Gospels. Jesus is baptized by John, and he is tempted by Satan in the desert. Then the proclamation of the kingdom begins in earnest.

In the Gospel of Luke, Jesus' public ministry began at home in Nazareth when he went to the synagogue on the Sabbath:

The scroll of the prophet Isaiah was given to him. He unrolled the scroll and found the place where it was written: "The Spirit of the Lord is upon me, because he has anointed me to bring good news to the poor. He has sent me to proclaim release to the captives and recovery of sight to the blind, to let the oppressed go free, to proclaim the year of the Lord's favor." And he rolled up the scroll, gave it back to the attendant, and sat down. The eyes of all in the synagogue were fixed on him. Then he began to say to them, "Today this scripture has been fulfilled in your hearing." (Luke 4:17–21)

Notice how Jesus refers to himself as the "anointed" one. It is an extraordinary claim! In the Hebrew Scriptures, the prophets announced that the Spirit of the Lord would rest on the hoped-for Messiah for his saving mission. The descent of the Holy Spirit on Jesus at his baptism by John was the sign that he is the "one who is to come," the Messiah, the Son of God. He was conceived of the Holy Spirit; his whole life and mission are carried out in total communion with the Holy Spirit given by the Father without measure.

The Hebrew word *messiah* means "anointed one," and it is translated into Greek by the word *christos*. *Christ* means the "anointed one." It is not Jesus' second name, as some mistakenly presume! No, Christ means "anointed one" and Christians are the "anointed ones."

Anointing with oil is a very ancient and important symbol in the Judeo-Christian tradition. It is interesting to note that the Jews anointed only two categories of people: priests and kings. In contrast to the Jewish practice, early Christians and the Church today anoint everyone in baptism and confirmation as sharing in the priestly, prophetic, and kingly life of Christ. This is the foundation of the ministry of all members of the Church. We are Christians; we are anointed ones, sharing in the messianic mission of Christ.

Through the power of the Holy Spirit, we, who are baptized and confirmed, are anointed to proclaim the kingdom of God.

The oil we use is called chrism. It is a mixture of olive oil and perfumed balsam. The chrism used in the sacraments is blessed by the bishop at the Chrism Mass during Holy Week. Its perfume reminds us of our dignity as daughters and sons of God who are loved. The anointing "christifies" us; it bestows the fullness of the Spirit, which makes us cry out "Abba, Father" and strengthens us to confess the name of Christ boldly.

This is the heart of confirmation no matter how or when it is conferred: infant, adolescent, or adult. Those who are confirmed receive the Spirit of the Lord to proclaim the kingdom of God. "Incorporated into Christ's Mystical Body through Baptism and strengthened by the power of the Holy Spirit through Confirmation, they are assigned to the apostolate by the Lord Himself. They are consecrated for the royal priesthood and the holy people (cf. 1 Peter 2:4–10) not only that they may offer spiritual sacrifices in everything they do but also that they may witness to Christ throughout the world."[2]

While the issues around the celebration of confirmation are often presented as a liturgical crisis, they also present us with pastoral possibilities and opportunities as we seek to understand the mission of the Church. All sacraments, confirmation included, are expressions of our wish to be disciples of Jesus Christ. Without that desire, implicit or explicit, we reduce these saving rites to magic moments, photo opportunities, and socially accepted excuses for family gatherings. Sacraments, the tradition tells us, are signs and causes. As such, they manifest our desire to be one with Christ in his Church. To celebrate one of these rites of the Church is to express our longing to enter more fully into the life of Christ so that we can give witness to his grace and power in the world. Confirmation is the sacrament of the Spirit that anoints us to participate in the saving mission of Christ the Lord. Before we celebrate it, we need to provoke an interest in discipleship and mission. That, Pope Francis noted during his pastoral visit to Brazil, is one of the great challenges facing the Church today.

CONVERSATION QUESTIONS

1. How does the sacrament of confirmation reflect the function of the Holy Spirit in our faith life?

2. Which of the gifts of the Holy Spirit are most important in your everyday life? How can you best respond to them?

3. What are some of the ways your local community might better proclaim and work for the realization of God's reign? How does confirmation help us to be agents of God's reign?

4. How does your parish celebrate confirmation as a community? How might you work with your pastor to improve the role confirmation plays in your parish?

5. In your opinion, what are some of the most important ways to prepare for confirmation?

6. As a "confirmed" Catholic, how can you give vibrant and public witness to your Christian faith?

EUCHARIST

✝

1322 The holy Eucharist completes Christian initiation. Those who have been raised to the dignity of the royal priesthood by Baptism and configured more deeply to Christ by Confirmation participate with the whole community in the Lord's own sacrifice by means of the Eucharist.

1323 "At the Last Supper, on the night he was betrayed, our Savior instituted the Eucharistic sacrifice of his Body and Blood. This he did in order to perpetuate the sacrifice of the cross throughout the ages until he should come again, and so to entrust to his beloved Spouse, the Church, a memorial of his death and resurrection: a sacrament of love, a sign of unity, a bond of charity, a Paschal banquet 'in which Christ is consumed, the mind is filled with grace, and a pledge of future glory is given to us.'"[1]

THE LITURGY OF THE EUCHARIST

COMMON PREFACE IV

It is truly right and just, our duty and our salvation,
always and everywhere to give you thanks,
Lord, holy Father, almighty and eternal God.
For, although you have no need of our praise,
yet our thanksgiving is itself your gift,
since our praises add nothing to your greatness,
but profit us for salvation,
through Christ our Lord.
And so, in company with the choirs of Angels,
we praise you, and with joy we proclaim:
Holy, Holy, Holy Lord God of hosts…

EUCHARISTIC PRAYER III

You are indeed Holy, O Lord,
and all you have created rightly gives you praise,
for through your Son our Lord Jesus Christ,
by the power and working of the Holy Spirit,
you give life to all things and make them holy,
and you never cease to gather a people to yourself,
so that from the rising of the sun to its setting
a pure sacrifice may be offered to your name.

Therefore, O Lord, we humbly implore you:
by the same Spirit graciously make holy
these gifts we have brought to you for consecration,
that they may become the Body and + Blood
of your Son our Lord Jesus Christ,
at whose command we celebrate these mysteries.

For on the night he was betrayed
he himself took bread,
and, giving you thanks, he said the blessing,
broke the bread and gave it to his disciples, saying:

TAKE THIS, ALL OF YOU, AND EAT OF IT,
FOR THIS IS MY BODY,
WHICH WILL BE GIVEN UP FOR YOU.

In a similar way, when supper was ended,
he took the chalice,
and, giving you thanks, he said the blessing,
and gave the chalice to his disciples, saying:

TAKE THIS, ALL OF YOU, AND DRINK FROM IT,
FOR THIS IS THE CHALICE OF MY BLOOD,
THE BLOOD OF THE NEW AND ETERNAL
　　　COVENANT,
WHICH WILL BE POURED OUT FOR YOU AND
　　　FOR MANY
FOR THE FORGIVENESS OF SINS.
DO THIS IN MEMORY OF ME.

The mystery of faith.

We proclaim your Death, O Lord,
and profess your Resurrection
until you come again.

Or:

When we eat this Bread and drink this Cup,
we proclaim your Death, O Lord,
until you come again.

Or:

Save us, Savior of the world,
for by your Cross and Resurrection
you have set us free.

Therefore, O Lord, as we celebrate the memorial
of the saving Passion of your Son,
his wondrous Resurrection
and Ascension into heaven,
and as we look forward to his second coming,
we offer you in thanksgiving
this holy and living sacrifice.

Look, we pray,
upon the oblation of your Church
and, recognizing the sacrificial Victim
by whose death you willed to reconcile us to yourself,
grant that we,
who are nourished by the Body and Blood of your Son
and filled with his Holy Spirit,
may become one body, one spirit in Christ.

May he make of us
an eternal offering to you,
so that we may obtain an inheritance with your elect,
especially with the most Blessed Virgin Mary, Mother
    of God,
with blessed Joseph, her Spouse,
with your blessed Apostles and glorious Martyrs
(with Saint N., the Saint of the day or Patron Saint)
and with all the Saints,
on whose constant intercession in your presence
we rely for unfailing help.

May this Sacrifice of our reconciliation,
we pray, O Lord,
advance the peace and salvation of all the world.
Be pleased to confirm in faith and charity
your pilgrim Church on earth,
with your servant Francis our Pope
and N. our Bishop, [and his assistant Bishops]
the Order of Bishops, all the clergy,
and the entire people you have gained for your own.

Listen graciously to the prayers of this family,
whom you have summoned before you:
in your compassion, O merciful Father,
gather to yourself all your children
scattered throughout the world.

† To our departed brothers and sisters
and to all who were pleasing to you
at their passing from this life,
give kind admittance to your kingdom.
There we hope to enjoy for ever the fullness of your
        glory
through Christ our Lord,
through whom you bestow on the world all that is
        good. †

Through him, and with him, and in him,
O God, almighty Father,
in the unity of the Holy Spirit,
all glory and honor is yours,
for ever and ever.

R. **Amen**.

8. Eucharist
The Many-Faceted Jewel
JOHN F. BALDOVIN, SJ

O sacred banquet!
in which Christ is received,
the memory of his Passion is renewed,
the mind is filled with grace,
and a pledge of future glory to us is given.
Alleluia

—Antiphon for the Feast of the Body and Blood of Christ

With these beautiful, poetic words, the great medieval theologian Saint Thomas Aquinas summed up the centrality of the Eucharist. The Eucharist is indeed the center of our lives quite simply because Christ himself is the center of our lives—not only the Lord Jesus who lived, taught, healed, was crucified, and raised from the dead two thousand years ago; not only the Christ whose saving and self-giving sacrifice we are mysteriously attached to every time we celebrate; not only the Christ whose bodily presence sustains us week by week (or even day by day); but also the Christ who beckons us forth to our ultimate vocation, living with him in the glory of the Father and the Holy Spirit.

For Catholics, and indeed for a great many Christians, the Eucharist is one of the most important and vital aspects of the faith. There is a story told of Christians on trial in an early third-century persecution of the church at Abitina in North Africa. The judges clearly thought the Christians were out of their minds because they were willing to die for what they believed in, but they showed that they weren't dying for a set of ideas as much as for the Lord himself when they responded, "But we cannot live without what we do on the Lord's Day." In other words, "we cannot live without our weekly celebration of the Eucharist." We clearly need to regain a sense of the importance and centrality of the Eucharist today, especially when so many Catholics regard the Sunday Eucharist as an option rather than a matter of life or death.

Much wonderful theology with regard to the Eucharist has been done within the Roman Catholic tradition, but I think it's important to recognize how significant the Eucharist is for so many Christians: Orthodox, Anglican, and Protestant. The ecumenical importance of the Eucharist can be discerned in a very important convergence (not yet consensus!) document published by the Faith and Order Commission of the World Council of Churches more than thirty years ago: "Baptism, Eucharist, and Ministry" (BEM). That document lays out a remarkable agreement achieved by Catholic, Orthodox, Anglican, and Protestant scholars.[1] It presents the Eucharist under five headings:

1. Thanksgiving to the Father

2. Memorial of the Son

3. Invocation of the Holy Spirit

4. Communion of the Faithful

5. Meal of the Kingdom

As all of our eucharistic prayers reveal, the main verb governing what we do at Mass is "to give thanks." Gratitude for what God has done for us in making us (creation) and saving us (redemption) is always at the forefront in our worship. That's why we can make "Eucharist" even when we celebrate a funeral. Formal Christian prayer has traditionally been directed to the Father, but it is done through Christ, because in the Eucharist (as well as all of our liturgical prayer) it is the paschal mystery (Christ's living, dying, and rising) that gives us access to the one he called *Abba*. Memorial means that we act out the pattern of Christ's person and acting for us as we repeat his actions at the Last Supper:

1. Taking—Presentation of the gifts

2. Blessing—Eucharistic Prayer

3. Breaking—Fraction

4. Giving—Communion

But the "we" has to be qualified by the fact that we can do nothing of worth without the empowerment of the Holy Spirit. That is why in all of our Eucharistic Prayers since Vatican II, the invocation (or *epiclesis*) of the Holy Spirit has been made explicit: "Therefore, O Lord, we humbly implore you: By the same Spirit graciously make holy these gifts we have brought to you for consecration, of your Son our Lord Jesus that they may become the Body and Blood of your Son our Lord Jesus Christ, at whose command we celebrate these mysteries." And so BEM alerts us to the fact that all three Persons of the Holy Trinity are involved in our Eucharist, and as the Body of Christ, the Church is involved as well. We often forget that the ultimate purpose of the Eucharist is not only the transformation of the bread and wine into the true body and blood of the Lord, but also *our transformation* into his one Body, the Church. BEM also reminds us that the Eucharist is the foretaste of the meal of God's kingdom. This generous self-giving and sharing of the Lord with us looks forward to the kingdom—to the final realization of God's plan. And so the Eucharist has profound ecclesial and ethical implications.

Consequently, the Eucharist is like a precious jewel. We cannot appreciate it by looking at it from only one angle or in only one light. We need to turn it now this way, now that, now in this light and then in another in order to begin to comprehend its true beauty. Furthermore, in order to appreciate it fully, we need to celebrate it well, in faith-filled communities with good pastoral leadership. It's also important to recognize that much of the meaning of the Eucharist is communicated through poetry, art, and music, all of which transcend simple, rational explanation.

The Eucharist indeed encompasses many facets of our Christian lives: the sense that God is truly with us; the challenge to participate in God's self-offering; the growth and true nourishment of our children; the awesome challenge to make gratitude (thanksgiving, *Eucharist*) the most significant element in our lives; the call to act morally and justly in our world; and the invitation to let Christ break down the barriers that divide us and to become what we truly are, as Saint Augustine so wonderfully says, the Body of Christ.

9. Being Kept by the Eucharist

CARDINAL SEÁN PATRICK O'MALLEY, OFM CAP

When I was bishop in the West Indies, the island where I lived had the oldest synagogue in the Western Hemisphere. It had been built by Sephardic Jews in what was then the Danish West Indies. One day the rabbi invited me to take a tour of the synagogue. It was a lovely old West Indian building with sand on the floor. In the ark was a magnificent ancient Torah scroll that had been brought there by the Sephardic Jews. As I walked around the synagogue, I picked up a prayer book that just happened to open to an ancient Jewish prayer that began with the words, "More than Israel has kept the Sabbath, the Sabbath has kept Israel." I was amazed. And I said to myself that the same is true for us of the New Covenant. More than we have kept the Sunday Mass obligation, it has kept us a people focused on God, united to one another and with a sense of mission.

Recently, I was at a benefit dinner. At this particular event a principal from a Catholic high school was being honored. In his acceptance speech he said, "I grew up in a family where going to Mass on Sunday was about as optional as breathing." The statement got quite a rise out of the audience, because I believe many of us could identify with those words. And it wasn't a matter of authoritarian parents, necessarily, or social pressure, but rather a sense of how important the Sunday Eucharist is for our own identity and survival.

In his *First Apologia*, addressed to the Emperor Antoninus and to the senate of Rome, Saint Justin proudly described the Christian practice of the Sunday assembly. During the persecution of Diocletian, those assemblies were banned with the greatest severity. Many Christians were courageous enough to defy the imperial decree and accepted death rather than miss the Sunday Eucharist. One of the responses of the accused, Emeritus, who declared that Christians had met in his house, has been often quoted. When he was asked why he violated the emperor's command, he said, "*Sine dominico non possumus*"—in other words, "We can't live without Sunday."

As a seminarian I remember reading an interview with Flannery O'Connor. She was asked what it was like to grow up Catholic in the South. Obviously, there were few Catholics there, particularly in those days, and many prejudices against Catholics. In this interview, Flannery O'Connor talks about her best friend from her childhood—a little Baptist girl. Flannery kept inviting her to accompany her to Mass. Finally, the little girl got permission from her mom to go to Mass with Flannery. Flannery couldn't wait for the Mass to be over so she could ask her, "Well, what did you think? What did you think?" And the little girl said, "Wow. You Catholics really have something special. The sermon was so boring. The music was so bad. The priest was mumbling in that language nobody could understand. And all those people were there." Obviously, they were not there to be entertained. And I'm sure that most of them there were there because *sine dominico non potuerunt*. The truth is that the Catholic Church sprang up around the Eucharist. Christ commanded us—do this in memory of me. Ever since, we have been doing this—celebrating his Eucharist; changing bread and wine into his body and blood so that the Good Shepherd can continue to feed his flock.

On one Mission Sunday, by chance the Gospel was the text of the Great Commandments. I fear often that when we think of Christian charity and Christian love and love of neighbor, we think only of feeding the hungry, caring for the sick and the elderly, providing for the homeless and the poor. However, if we truly love our neighbor, we will likewise be very concerned that there are many people who are spiritually homeless, spiritually hungry, spiritually imprisoned, and spiritually sick. The Church exists to evangelize—to announce the good news of God's love and desire that we follow him as part of his people. Discipleship is never a solo flight, but rather an adventure that we live together. At the heart of that adventure is the eucharistic banquet, where Calvary and the Last Supper become present in our life and our history.

When I was a young priest in Washington, the Kennedy Center was dedicated. Jackie Kennedy had invited Leonard Bernstein to compose a piece for the opening performance, and he wrote his famous Mass. One scene in particular was the source of much comment at the time. At a very emotional climax, with growing cacophony of the choruses, the celebrant, in a furious rage, hurls the chalice to the floor. The image of Bernstein's Mass resonates with the story of Moses going up Mount Sinai to receive the tablets of the law. And when he came down and saw the community in disarray and worshiping the golden calf, he cast the tablets on the ground and broke them. Bernstein, a Jew, had no doubt incorporated this image into his Mass, having the celebrant cast down the chalice—being like Moses smashing the tablets. When people are not worshiping God, they begin to worship the golden calf. They begin to find many false gods—money, power, and pleasure among them. If we love God with our whole mind and our whole heart and our whole strength, we must not turn our back on his commandment to keep holy the Lord's Day.

In a society that is highly individualistic, as described in Professor Putnam's *Bowling Alone*, in which he shows how each successive generation of Americans spends more time alone—eating alone, living alone, spending hours alone before a television or a computer screen—we must communicate that discipleship means being part of Jesus' family, part of the community. In a culture that's addicted to entertainment, some Christian churches have turned themselves into entertainment centers. In the Eucharist we have something much more important than entertainment. We have love taken to the extreme. Our God has made a gift of himself to us, and God invites us to wash each other's feet and to make a gift of our lives to God and to one another.

An important way to measure our success in evangelizing and forming a new generation of disciples has to be how faithful we are to the Sunday Eucharist—with the strength that comes from the word of God, which we break open at Mass, and the community, from the witness of our brothers and sisters in the faith. It's hard to imagine how someone can persevere in a life of discipleship. The metaphor of the vine and the branches is most apt. A branch cut off from the vine cannot survive very long. And so, in today's world, where the values of the gospel are often dismissed out of hand, where religion is trivialized, and where political correctness trumps even the supremacy of conscience—in such a society, only those Catholics who pray and come to Mass are going to persevere in their vocation to be Jesus' disciples in the Catholic Church. Our celebration of the Eucharist—the sacrifice of the Mass—is for us as Catholics a family meal. It is there that we experience God's love. We learn our own identity—who we are, why we're in this world, and what we have to do with our lives. Not going to Mass is to stop breathing—to stop breathing the life of the body of Christ.

Our ideal is to make the Sunday Eucharist our Sabbath—a great school of charity, justice, and peace. As we read in the encyclical *Deus Domini*, the presence of the risen Lord in the midst of his people becomes an undertaking of solidarity—a compelling force for inner renewal, an inspiration to change the structures of sin in which individuals, communities, and at times, entire peoples are entangled. Far from being an escape, the Christian Sunday is a prophecy inscribed on time itself—a prophecy obliging the faithful to follow in the footsteps of the One who came to preach the good news to the poor, to proclaim release to captives, and give new sight to the blind, to set at liberty those who are oppressed, and to proclaim the acceptable year of the Lord.

For each of us, Sunday is the day of the resurrection. On that first Easter, Jesus appeared to the two disciples on the road to Emmaus. The disciples were confused, hurt, and full of fear and doubts. They were trying to determine what to make of the death of Jesus and the empty tomb. They were discussing these developments when Jesus, whom they did not recognize, drew near and began to speak with them. When they reached the village, they invited Jesus to stay with them. Saint Luke says that at that moment Jesus made as if he were going to continue on his journey. It was their invitation that brought Jesus to the table. The Lord is always waiting for us to invite him into our lives. When they sat down for the evening meal, Jesus took the bread, blessed it, broke it, and gave it to them. At that point the disciples recognized Jesus. Suddenly, he vanished, but the bread remained. Then the disciples rushed back to Jerusalem to tell the apostles that Jesus had truly risen and appeared to them.

We, too, live in times when many people are confused and hurt and full of fear. Jesus wants to meet us in the same way he met the disciples on the road to Emmaus. Like them, we will recognize Jesus and encounter him most profoundly in the breaking of the bread at Mass. The Eucharist is the fulfillment of Jesus' promise to be with us until the end of time. I pray that our love for the Mass and the eucharistic amazement will increase so that our hearts will be burning within us when we hear the Sacred Scriptures proclaimed and observe the breaking of the bread.

Let us do what those disciples on the road to Emmaus did. Let us rush out to tell the world that Christ is alive and that our family must gather at the Lord's Table to experience God's love, to learn our own identity, and to fulfill our mission together—to say to the world that we have seen the Lord and have recognized him in the breaking of the bread.

10. The Ministries of the Eucharist

JOYCE ANN ZIMMERMAN, CPPS

Some of us are old enough to remember back a half century before the liturgical renewal of the Second Vatican Council. *Ministry* wasn't a word bantered around much then. The notion of ministry was much simpler: the priest ministered on behalf of the people. He offered Mass for us. The only other folks evident who were "ministering" were altar servers, ushers, and the choir. And these ministries were filled by boys and men (at one time women were not even permitted in parish choirs). Observing any parish Mass today, we find a variety of people doing various ministries during Mass—boys and girls, men and women. However, multiplying people and ministries doesn't always get us where we need to be. Let us reflect more on the ministries of the Eucharist and the people who undertake them.

MINISTRY AS FIRST *BEING*, THEN *DOING*

We begin our reflection not with the priest or any of the other ministries, but by making a critical distinction. The ministries of the Eucharist are, to some extent, about getting a "job" done. The Readings need to be proclaimed, Christ's body and blood need to be given, and so on. Each minister, in fact, has a job to do, but if that were all there is to it, there might be better ways to go about ministering than forming and scheduling people, which can sometimes be a time-consuming effort. To move from getting a job done to truly being a minister means that underlying the *doing* must be a *being*. In other words, each ministry has a spirituality in which it is grounded. When the minister lives the particular spirituality, he or she truly ministers; if not, he or she is simply getting a job done.

Being the ministry comes first. What we mean by this is that we must live our baptismal identity—to be the Body of Christ— from the perspective of the particular ministry we have embraced. Basic to this kind of living is the rhythm of the paschal mystery. While preparing to minister and while ministering during Mass, we are visible icons of Christ's death and resurrection, of his self-emptying and exaltation. *Being* the ministry means we live it before we come to the celebration of Mass.

Similarly, *doing* the ministry is important. No matter what our particular ministry, we participate in all of Mass (not just while we are doing our ministry) in such a way that we *model* the rhythm of the paschal mystery from our lived experience of it. Furthermore, *doing* our ministry is a concrete way to share with our sisters and brothers in Christ the unique gift given us by the Holy Spirit at baptism, that is, to build up the Body of Christ.

Always, both the *being* and the *doing* of our ministry bring us to Christ. It is Christ's mystery we celebrate at Mass; it is Christ who is present in continual self-giving; it is Christ who is present within us and to us, and who leads us ever deeper into the mystery of salvation.

Ministry of the Assembly

The most important ministry during Mass is that of the gathered assembly. The liturgical assembly manifests the Church, the Body of Christ, in its fullness. As *liturgical* assembly it enacts the paschal mystery and thus continues Christ's ongoing work of salvation. When we gather as liturgical assembly, we call to mind and live out our identity as Christians to be the Church, the Body of Christ. We are Church made visible. We are the members of Christ's body now gathered around Christ, the head of his body.

What we *do* is important: we sit, stand, and kneel; we sing and pray; we give and receive; we interact with others and encounter God. All this *doing*, however, is empty—is going through mere motions—if we are not also *being*. Our *being* the assembly requires other-centeredness, surrendering to God's transforming action during Mass, accepting diversity, recognizing each member's place and role in diversity, focusing on our common identity under Jesus Christ, committing ourselves to celebrating Mass wholeheartedly, hearing the dismissal at the end of Mass as a command from Christ to live what we have celebrated.

Ministry of the Priest-Presider

The priest no longer *does* something *for* us. His role is to be the visible presence of Christ, the head of the Church. He speaks and prays both for Christ and for the assembly. The priest is one who leads us to be assembly, the Church before God participating in the perpetual sacrifice of Christ's self-giving. What the priest *does* is important: he leads and models, he sings and prays, he preaches and teaches. His *being* priest requires that he live Christ's self-giving, that he knows where he is leading the assembly, that he prays with an open heart, that he practices in everything he does encountering Christ, of whom he is the visible presence. The priest is to be Christ not only during Mass; being Christ at all times is who he is as a baptized Christian and member of the assembly. He is not apart from the assembly, but one with the assembly.

Ministry of the Deacon

Historically, the primary role of the deacon is not liturgical, but one of service. Certainly, however, the deacon does have a liturgical role: he proclaims the Gospel, receives the gifts from the assembly (both the bread and wine as well as the gifts for those in need), and dismisses the assembly to live what it has celebrated. The deacon's liturgical role is directly connected with his service to the community: by attending to those in need, he is making the gospel visible in everyday living; by receiving the gifts from the assembly, he is reminding himself and others that the community has an obligation to those suffering and in need; by dismissing the assembly, he is inviting them to imitate his self-giving, Christlike service.

Ministry of Lector

The lector is one who proclaims God's word to the assembly. To this end, the lector must *be* a living word; one cannot proclaim what one does not live. The word burns within the heart of the lector so that, like Paul, the lector can say, "Not I, but Christ in me!" This burning of the word distinguishes reading from proclaiming. One reads words with the head. One proclaims God's word from the heart, informed by one's life. In order to *be* the ministry of lector, one must regularly and often ponder God's word, listen for God's word in prayer and through others, pray the scriptures (engage in *lectio divina* or "divine reading"), practice charity and "elegance" in speech, praise God often and everywhere. The lector is one who *becomes* God's word, *lives* God's word, *loves* God's word.

Extraordinary Minister of Holy Communion

The extraordinary minister of holy communion is one who—first and foremost—proclaims by his or her very life the belief that he or she is the Body of Christ. This minister is gracious (grace-filled, gift-giving) in distributing communion at Mass and compassionate when bringing communion to the sick and homebound. By the sheer goodness of life, this minister brings Christ's presence to others—the Blessed Sacrament as well as the risen presence of Christ in the Church. In order to minister in this way, the extraordinary minister of holy communion strives to be truly present to others, believes self and others are truly the Body of Christ, models this in life, is comfortable looking others "in the eye," is generous with a genuine sharing of self, fosters the dignity of others by gentleness and personal warmth, and puts others ahead of self.

Ministry of Music

Through music, these ministers (assembly, psalmist, cantor, choir, music director, presider, accompanists) support the unfolding of the liturgical action and help the assembly enter into and respond to that action as the one Body of Christ. Singing at Mass is not simply vocalizing; it is joining one's self to the heavenly choir before the throne of God, offering God perpetual praise and thanksgiving. To this end, the music minister must see *self* as the primary musical instrument, *hear* the rhythm of the paschal mystery in the rhythm of the music, embody the sound of surrender. The music minister is a living song of God's mercy and compassion, faithfulness and care, goodness and graciousness.

Ministry of Hospitality

Hospitality ministers welcome the members of the Body of Christ who are gathering for liturgy as sisters and brothers in Christ (greeters, ushers), assist them with any needs (greeters, ushers), attend to the good order of the sacred space (environment ministers, sacristans), and assist other ministers (acolytes or altar ministers). As such, this ministry calls forth from those assembling a deep sense of identity (Body of Christ) and "being at home." Hospitality ministers help the assembly members make the transition from the cares of daily life to surrendering to the majesty and mystery of divine presence. They help promote unity within the community, help the people gather to surrender to the Spirit's transforming power, and help the assembly *be* Church-made-visible. In order to do this from within their very being, hospitality ministers present a joyful, happy disposition during liturgy as well as in their daily living. They show genuine care and concern for others; are prayerfully "at home" in God's house; are hospitable in personal life and generous with home and belongings; are gracious and welcoming when greeting others at church and in daily living; are inclusive of everyone; are quick to compliment and forgive, surrender and serve; and are humble and generous. Hospitality ministers are oriented toward others.

All these ministries of the Eucharist require far more than getting a job done. They require eucharistic daily living expressed by self-giving for the good of others. This is what the risen Christ gives to us in his own body and blood; this is what we give to each other as members of the Body of Christ.

11. The Word in Worship

KATHLEEN HUGHES, RSCJ

About fifty years ago, with a single sentence, an extraordinary transformation of the Sunday Eucharist was launched by the bishops gathered at the Second Vatican Council (1962–65). The bishops decreed, "The Order of Mass is to be revised in a way that will bring out more clearly the intrinsic nature and purpose of its several parts, as also the connection between them, and will more readily achieve the devout, active participation of the faithful."[1]

The elders among us will remember that, prior to Vatican II, there were three principal parts of the Eucharist, namely, the Offertory, Consecration, and Communion. In a way, the reading of the word of God was like an appendage. Certainly, at every Sunday celebration of the Eucharist, an Epistle and a Gospel were read and a sermon nearly always followed, but often the sermon had little to do with the word that had just been proclaimed or the sacramental act that followed. A sign of the cross began and ended the sermon, suggesting symbolically that this was an independent ritual unit, like a time out, before the real business of worship began. The intrinsic nature and purpose of the word of God and the connection of the Liturgy of the Word with the balance of the celebration were completely opaque except, perhaps, to those who knew something of the historical development of the church's worship and the early fusion of a service of the word with the breaking of the bread.

All that changed with Vatican II's recovery of that more ancient pattern of word and Eucharist, the two principal parts of every celebration. These central elements are introduced and concluded with simple but important rituals that serve to gather the community for worship and to send them to be God's heart in a world in need of healing and hope. The balance of this reflection considers the intrinsic nature and purpose of four ritual moments and their inherent relationship to one other, highlighting in the process the key role of the homily (and the homilist) in achieving both the connection among these elements and, more important, the active participation of the faithful in the entire event of worship. These ritual moments are the Introductory Rites, the Liturgy of the Word, the Liturgy of the Eucharist, and the Concluding Rites.

THE INTRODUCTORY RITES

According to the *General Instruction of the Roman Missal,* the rites that precede the Liturgy of the Word (Entrance, Greeting, Penitential Act, Kyrie, Gloria, and Collect) have as their purpose to establish communion among those who gather and to prepare them to enter into the celebration of word and Eucharist.[2] These gathering rites are not insignificant, but perhaps more critical in forging communion is the presider's thoughtful attention to those who have come together and the particular affinities of mind and heart they share.

A 2013 document of the United States Conference of Catholic Bishops, "Preaching the Mystery of Faith," names some of the issues that have transformed the makeup of the Sunday assembly in the last several decades: there is far greater cultural diversity in the assembly; those who gather are deeply influenced by the secularization of the culture; there is a fair amount of disaffection with the Church and less inclination to grant it moral authority; and many of those who gather have yet to be catechized.[3] Furthermore, those in the Sunday assembly are deeply affected by the ubiquitous news stream bringing tragedy and triumph from half a world away. They are of a variety of political persuasions and ecclesial "tribes." Seasons and holidays color their experience; local and familial events preoccupy them. These are the people to whom the Liturgy of the Word is addressed. Perhaps what actually binds them together is a deep longing for a word that will touch and transform all these preoccupations with a message of compassion and hope.

THE LITURGY OF THE WORD

In order that the treasures of the Bible might be "opened up more lavishly [and] a richer share in God's word [might] be provided for the faithful,"[4] Vatican II directed a complete revision of the Lectionary. Now, a three-year cycle of readings from Matthew, Mark, and Luke are read in turn, and the Gospel of John is proclaimed on most "high holy days" throughout the year. The First Reading harmonizes thematically with the Gospel, and a portion of a psalm provides the community an opportunity to respond. A Second Reading, from the Acts of the Apostles or other New Testament texts, is related to the First Reading and the Gospel during the major seasons of the Church year.

Rich fare, indeed, but for the homilist, a quandary: Where to begin? How to open up this banquet? How to address those gathered who ache to hear a word of nourishment for their lives? Thirty years ago the bishops of the United States published "Fulfilled in Your Hearing: The Homily in the Sunday Assembly," a document that examined the interrelationship of the assembly, the preacher, and the homily and then proposed a rigorous homiletic method of preparation in order that priests might fulfill their primary duty, namely, "the proclamation of the Gospel of

God to all."[5] The pastoral and practical insights of this document remain important and valid today. "Fulfilled in Your Hearing" was a groundbreaking document that truly assisted homilists in embracing their preaching role.

"Preaching the Mystery of Faith" has shifted the focus. It provides an extensive and powerful theology of the word of God, instilling in the reader the inescapable conclusion that, while homiletic techniques enhance preaching, it must first of all be grounded in a passion for the word of God. "Preaching the Mystery of Faith" imagines the transformation of preaching by homilies born and nurtured in the homilist's ever-deepening biblical spirituality. In fact, this document recommends the regular spiritual discipline of *lectio divina*,[6] an ancient exercise in which one listens deeply to the word of God "with the ear of the heart."[7] The Sunday Scriptures are read and reread; the homilist listens for God's word in these texts, at this moment in the community's life, for this particular community gathered, hoping that such faithful listening and prayerful preparation will make God's word come alive, will make our hearts burn within us, will help us recognize the person and work of Christ in establishing God's reign in our world, and will invite us to accept—indeed, embrace—our role in continuing Jesus' saving mission in our world.

Consequently, the homily must be born in prayer; it must be inspired and tested by the Spirit of God, and it must be a word of consolation and a word of challenge in the life of the homilist before it is offered to the assembly. Implicitly or explicitly, the Liturgy of the Word, culminating in the homily, calls for conversion in homilist and community alike.

THE LITURGY OF THE EUCHARIST

Indeed, it is that summons to conversion that leads us to turn to the table and to join ourselves to the life, death, and rising of Christ for the life of the world in the Eucharist. During the preparation rite we place ourselves with the gifts of bread and wine and beg that we, too, will be transformed into the body and blood of Christ just as truly as the bread and wine.

Then we tell the ancient story once again. We speak of God's mighty deeds in the history of salvation and of Jesus Christ, who moved among us doing good and revealing to us the face of God. We tell of how he went to death and how God raised him up as Lord of the living and the dead. We join ourselves with Christians across the world and with those who have gone before us in this great prayer of praise and thanksgiving. Once the story is complete, we receive him who, gradually and imperceptibly, transforms our words and deeds that we, too, become a revelation of God's face to our world.

CONCLUDING RITES

There is little left to do. The concluding rites draw our celebration to a close with a final prayer asking God's grace to live in the coming days what we have heard in the word and have promised with every amen we have uttered. Then we are blessed and sent, to "glorify the Lord by our lives."

The intrinsic nature and purpose of the elements of worship and their interconnection are simply and beautifully illustrated in the story of Jesus' post-resurrection appearance to the disciples on the road to Emmaus (Luke 24:13–35). As we noted in chapter 9, there is a meeting on the road of two disciples and a stranger, who helps them to understand the words of the prophets, and they find new meaning in the events they have experienced in Jerusalem. They are touched to the core; their hearts come alive again. Through the simple action of the breaking of bread, the disciples know Christ in a new way, and though he has vanished from their sight, they return without delay to Jerusalem to spread the astonishing news that they have seen the Lord.

All the elements of worship are there; the dynamic among them is transparent; the role of word and preaching is central; and the ultimate mission of the Christian could not be more simply stated.

12. Sacramental Real Presence

RODICA STOICOIU

In this brief chapter, we attempt to provide some basic concepts helpful in understanding sacramental real presence by looking at four areas: the understanding of the Eucharist in the earliest New Testament writings, how symbols are to be approached as the language of sacrament, the place of mystery in this expression of Christ's presence, and the role of transubstantiation in the explanation of sacramental real presence.

Why go to all this trouble? Remember that the celebration of the Eucharist is the most radical act for Catholics. It is the symbol of our unity with God and one another. It is the fullest expression of our identity, born in the waters of baptism and most wholly expressed around the table. Through it, we make known that we are the Body of Christ, a communion of persons—radically, socially, in the image of God. And through all of this we claim that Christ is truly, fully, really present. But what do we mean by this presence? This question is important on many levels—for catechesis, for the faith of all who celebrate the eucharistic liturgy, and for ecumenical dialogue, just to name a few. Hence, it would seem a credible project to understand more deeply the meaning behind this presence.

Of course, the place to begin is the New Testament. The earliest account of the Eucharist is that of Paul in First Corinthians. In this text he describes a eucharistic liturgy and gives a theology that challenges his community to live as Christ lived. Paul notes that he is passing on a tradition that he himself received, and he is asking the community at Corinth to make this tradition their own. "For I received from the Lord what I also handed on to you" (1 Cor 11:23). He is asking them through repeated celebrations of the Eucharist to appropriate its meaning and to make this meaning a part of their own lives, "For all who eat and drink without discerning the body, eat and drink judgment against themselves" (1 Cor 11:29). He is asking them to live what they celebrate: a life focused on caring for the poor and the needy, a life of inclusivity and radical egalitarianism.[1] Paul does not make a distinction between event (action) and object; it is all Eucharist, and Christ is present in it. That Christ was present was a given for Paul; how Christ was present is a question that would not have occurred to him.[2] His concern was on the Eucharist as an action of the community, one that forms it into the body of Christ through constant repetition. His focus was to make sure they celebrated well if it was truly to form and transform them into the Church, the ecclesial Body. From this we can say that there is a relation for Paul between the celebration of the sacrament of the Eucharist, the real presence of Christ in the Eucharist, and the presence of Christ in the ecclesial Body, the Church.[3] Paul's concerns are also our concerns. It is only in repeating the celebration of the Eucharist over and over again that we come to inculcate its meaning into our lives. It is only through repeated encounters with the Eucharist that we, too, make the connections among celebration, presence, and the Church. As David Power notes, "It is significant and needs to be signified that Jesus is present to his community in every action of word, prayer, and mutual charity, and in every exercise of the gifts of the Spirit. The ultimate symbolic expression of ecclesial being…is the reality of the body of the Lord around the communion table."[4]

Second, the sacramental real presence of Christ is communicated to us through symbols. You can think of symbols as the language that conveys sacrament. Always keep in mind that our eucharistic celebrations are part of a symbolic order rooted in a culture of specific symbols and rituals that sacramentally express the real presence of Christ. As is noted in the *Constitution on the Sacred Liturgy*, there are four modes of the presence of Christ in the eucharistic celebration: in the community celebrating, in the word proclaimed, in the priest presiding, and in a special way in the bread and the wine.[5] All four of these modes communicate Christ's presence symbolically. However, not everyone understands symbols the same way. Many are suspicious of symbols. They see them as something superficial, holding little to no meaning. You've probably heard the expression, "It's not real; it's just a symbol." The implication here is that symbols are the opposite of reality. This is not true. Since the reforms of Vatican II, we have been retrieving an understanding of symbol as that which is complex and multivocal, that is, with many levels of meaning. Symbols mediate and interpret our reality. They invite us to participate and enter into a deeper reality. They call us to become involved emotionally, intellectually, and morally. Symbols point us to the "other" encountered in the celebration of the sacraments.[6] They are multivalent, ambiguous, and very real. It is through repeated exposure to them that we come to a deeper experience of Christ's presence.

Our third concept is mystery. Indeed, the term *sacrament* (*sacramentum*) translates the Greek word *mysterion*, "mystery," at the heart of which is the basic symbol of Christian life, the touchstone from which all other symbols are to be interpreted: the life, death, and resurrection of Christ and our lives therein, the paschal mystery. Mystery and symbol are intimately connected. The ability of symbols to open us to the "other" allows us to enter into the mystery of sacramental real presence. This is possible because there is both a divine presence in these encounters, and also a divine absence. We come to experience the mystery at the heart of sacrament through symbols because they point to, yet cannot contain, the realities they communicate. There is always something absent in the indications symbols provide. This is their power. Nathan Mitchell argues that "the Catholic tradition has thus maintained (for nearly two millennia) that 'sacrament' both comforts us with presence and confronts us with an absence, an irreducible 'otherness,' a mystery."[7] Hence, our eucharistic symbols (word, action, event, object) are invitations into an experience of the transcendent. And there is a deeply relational dimension to this experience. Power presents this relational element as follows:

> When Christ is present to his people through the sacramental gift of his body and blood, the sacramental representation of this gift is the offer to a community, and includes the response to invitation, which is the communal eating and drinking at the one table, of the one loaf and the one cup.[8]

In the experience of sacramental real presence, the community moves in relationship into the presence of Christ through the Spirit. Through the experience of the eating and the drinking, we are drawn into the mystery of Christ, which itself as mystery can "redefine matter and reconfigure perception."[9] Sacramental real presence is truly mystery because it points to that which is both truly present but also truly absent; the Divine Mystery, the triune God.

Fourth, we need to know where transubstantiation fits into the picture. There was a time in our history when we emphasized an overly physical understanding of real presence. This happens when the relational, multivalent power of symbol is lost and replaced by allegory. When this occurs we move from "ambiguity to clarity...from revelation to explanation."[10] In so doing, we rob the symbol of its ability to communicate mystery. But we know that we are dealing not with the physical flesh of Christ "eaten by Christians, broken by the priest's hands," but with the sacramental real presence of Christ.[11] Transubstantiation is understood as a change in the substance of bread and wine, a change in the "definitive reality of what is present and presented in the sacrament," and this happens as a "result of the liturgical or sacramental action."[12] The bread and wine act within a symbolic construct, revealing a deeper reality. Does the concept of transubstantiation go far enough in explaining sacramental real presence today? It is one possible explanation that certainly counters the intensely physical realism of an earlier age, but it is limited. As Mitchell states, "Eucharistic real presence is not transubstantiation."[13] Transubstantiation specifically focuses on the objects of bread and wine. "The body of Christ offered to Christians in consecrated bread and wine is not some*thing* but some*one*. In the Eucharist, Christ is present not as an object to be admired but as a real person."[14] To speak of sacramental real presence is to encompass the full mystery of sacrament as event through word, action, and object. Ultimately, sacramental real presence must be understood as a totality of all of those.

From the early Church to today, we can understand that "the presence of Christ is given to the Church through the medium of narrative, blessing, bread and wine, eating and drinking, within a community of service."[15] Sacramental real presence encompasses word, event, and object. It is fundamentally relational, an event that draws us more and more fully into the mystery of God. "The body of Christ is not only *on* the table but *at* the table."[16] In the end we will be the ones who are changed through this sacramental encounter. We will, in the words of Saint Augustine, "become what we see, receive what we are." What are we? The Body of Christ, the Spirit-filled people of God.

13. The Eucharist and Sacrifice

CHELSEA KING

The general meaning of *sacrifice* has shifted and developed throughout the centuries, and today it carries with it a slightly negative connotation. To sacrifice something is to give it up for the sake of something greater. A woman sacrifices her career to raise her children; a straight-A student sacrifices a social life to achieve perfect scores; an athlete sacrifices physical comfort to win a race. Sacrifice indeed permeates our secular culture, but what about the religious sphere? Most people today do not resonate with the idea of a God who demands sacrifice to appease his wrath. It is hard to imagine a priest today offering a sacrifice to God whose offering brings about forgiveness and promotes a state of peace. Although it may seem like a distant and foreign concept, for any Catholic attending Mass these ancient sacrificial images, which seem so foreign, are actually closer than they appear to be. Walk into any Mass and you will hear the priest using phrases such as "sacrificial victim" and "we offer you his body and blood." Those in the pews even respond with, "May the Lord accept the sacrifice at your hands." It becomes increasingly difficult for an outsider (and perhaps even those reciting the prayer in Mass) to understand the meaning of these phrases in a world in which the very idea of human sacrifice instills moral disdain. Is the Catholic Mass any different from an archaic sacrificial institution?

First, it is important to recognize that the Eucharist is a sacrifice that is directly linked to the sacrifice of Christ on the cross. A proper understanding of the meaning of the salvific value of the cross and resurrection becomes necessary in order to understand how the Eucharist functions as a sacrifice today. Important questions for this discussion are: Did God demand that his Son be sacrificed to redeem humanity? Did God, upon seeing his Son on the cross expend the wrath that he had been reserving for us? What is it about an *innocent* death that forgives sins?

These questions are multifaceted and stem from a tension within Christianity between God's "justice" and God's "mercy." The Gospels shed light upon this tension and allow us to obtain a deeper understanding of the meaning of the cross. The most important theme throughout the Gospels, and one that all four have in common, is the *innocence* of Christ. Christ, while being judged by the Roman authorities as a criminal (crucifixion was reserved for criminals and revolutionaries against the Roman state), was innocent and did not deserve death. This emphasis on innocence is the first and essential difference between an ancient sense of human sacrifice and a Christian sense of sacrifice. In the ancient ritual of human sacrifice, sacrificial victims were "chosen by God" to be sacrificed. Their death would never be cast in terms of a murder or slaying of an innocent victim. The Gospels, on the other hand, make it clear that Christ was killed unjustly. There is thus a reversal and subversion of all forms of human sacrifice. We can say with certainty that God did not *demand* an innocent death in order to redeem humanity. However, here we have another seemingly unresolvable tension within the Christian tradition: The death of Christ was not necessary in order for God to forgive humanity, for the incarnation itself *presupposes* that God's offer of forgiveness is unconditional. But despite this, it is clear that God *still* desired that Jesus go to the cross.

There is one possible explanation, which in no way claims to provide a sufficient rationale for the cross. What is often overlooked in the resurrection accounts is the fact that Jesus, even though he had been murdered unjustly, never sought vengeance. Instead, he offered *forgiveness.* True reconciliation between humanity and God is found in that position of forgiveness. Human beings are violent creatures who have a distorted view of God, which has manifested itself in the belief that God is violent and in turn demands violence. Opposed to this human projection of who God is stands the risen Christ, whose glorious light of forgiveness illumines the darkness of the cross. In allowing himself to be killed by human beings in a way that appears to be justified to them, Christ allowed himself to be taken over momentarily by the violence of humanity. The Father asks the Son to go through with this event in order to *reveal* its injustice and our complicity in its violence. In his resurrection Christ's innocence is declared, but instead of seeking vengeance on his perpetrators, forgiveness presents itself and renders the violent tendencies within our hearts silent.

In receiving the Eucharist, in receiving this sacrificial victim who was in some sense sacrificed to *us,* there is hope that we can be transformed into Christ. His was a life marked by self-sacrifice, and in receiving his body and blood, we too can live a life marked by self-sacrifice, reconciliation, and *divine* justice. In this sense, the Mass, by employing ancient terminology, completely subverts the ancient understanding of human sacrifice and God. Divine justice shakes the very foundation of human justice to its core, rendering it void. Human justice demands vengeance, while divine justice offers forgiveness; its only demand is that we tear down the false idols of God once and for all.

14. The Feast of Corpus Christi

MARK RAVIZZA, SJ

Remember and do not forget how the Lord, your God, guided you through a vast and terrible desert and fed you with bread from heaven. (Deut 8:14–16)

The year I turned twelve, I was "sentenced" to spend my summer sorting nuts and bolts in the warehouse of Cupertino Electric. It was, for a young boy, mind-numbingly boring work. By the time 9:45 finally arrived—I usually started work around 9:00—an eternity seemed to have passed, and the hours of the day stretched endlessly before me like some vast and terrible desert, filled not with seraph serpents and scorpions, but with wirenuts, EMT connectors, and innumerable PVC couplings. In my despair my eyes looked continually to the heavens. I would like to say I was praying, but in fact I was scanning the skies for cigar smoke—a sign that my beloved grandfather was puffing his way to my salvation, lunch at Grandma's house. Once there, the ritual began: Grandma would don her old apron, lead me out to the garden, and there we would take from her carefully tended plants the beginnings of our lunch: red, ripe tomatoes, long green beans, sweet corn, zucchini blossoms. Back in the kitchen she would combine this harvest with food she had been slaving over all morning, while my grandfather and I—like good Italian men—sat at the table and watched her cook. Always before eating, we said a blessing, giving thanks and praise to God for the gifts placed before us on the table. Then my grandmother would break the bread, divide the food, and give it to us to eat. While we ate, my grandparents told me stories. Stories of my dad growing up, of the practical jokes he played on my aunt, of my Italian ancestors coming to this country, of working on the ranch, cutting cots in the summer, putting smudge pots out when the weather got cold, of the hard times during the depression. And somewhere during the meal—usually as I asked for my third piece of apricot pie—my grandmother would say, "So you like it?" And when I answered, "Yes," she would deliver the punch line: "Well, you're a Ravizza." The trap had been sprung. I had implicated myself. I was a Ravizza. The stories I heard were my story; the food I loved made me one with those who loved me.

Years later I realized that my grandmother was doing more than giving me lunch each day. She was giving me an identity—telling me who I was and where I came from, to whom I belonged and how I should live. At the end of those lunches I felt grateful. I felt as if I were part of something larger than myself, that I had received a great gift and the only appropriate response was to want to return that gift by imitating the lives of those who had given me so much. I was a Ravizza, and the least I could do was to endure another afternoon sorting locknuts in the warehouse.

Remember and do not forget how the Lord, your God, guided you through a vast and terrible desert and fed you with bread from heaven.

If, as Genesis tells us, we are made in the image of God, then what is most human gives us a glimpse of what is divine. My grandmother wanted to pour her life into me. There is no nobler yearning of the human heart than longing to give ourselves to those we love. God perfects and completes this yearning. God takes it literally. As Jesus says, "I am the living bread come down from heaven"—the food he offers is his very self, body and blood. What my grandmother did for me all those years ago, God wants to do today: to pour God's life into us; to feed us when we are in need; to show us to whom we are connected and how we should live. This is what we celebrate here.

In a moment we will gather at the table and hear one more story. How on the night he was betrayed, Jesus took bread, said a blessing, broke the bread, and gave it to his friends. Four actions: take, bless, break, and give. These four actions summarize Jesus' entire life. For he takes all he is, his very life, from the Father; he blesses the Father for that gift through his thanks and praise. He does not cling or grasp to what he has received but allows himself to be broken so that his life may be given to others—he suffers for curing those who suffer; he is cast out for eating with prostitutes and outcasts; he is charged as a sinner for forgiving sin; and in the end, he is imprisoned for setting others free and crucified so that we might live. Take, bless, break, and give. If Jesus' promise to feed us with his very self has any credibility, it is because his whole life evinces this pattern of self-donation.

As we retell this ancient story, it becomes our story; the past tense suddenly becomes present—after hearing that Jesus took, blessed, broke, and gave the bread, we hear the words "take this all of you...do this in memory of me," and there is no one here to do so but us. The trap has been sprung. We are implicated, for we cannot receive such a gift without wanting, without needing, to offer something in return. As any lover knows, one does not accept the heart of another lightly, for an offering of such value demands an equal sharing of love in return. And how much more this gift of God's very self? The only appropriate response is to become what we behold, to imitate the pattern of Jesus' life by allowing our lives to be taken, blessed, broken, and given. We must imitate the sacrifice we receive.

It is not a popular word these days—*sacrifice*. Yet, without it our loves remain infatuations and our commitments, unrealized dreams. I know a man who came here from another country and sacrificed for the last twenty-five years cleaning toilets so that his children would have a better life. There is the mother who sacrifices her career to spend more time with her family; the Silicon Valley employee exhausted after work who goes each week to read for the blind; the grandmother who struggles through the pain of arthritic hands to write a note to her grandson. This is the best of who we are. The Eucharist reminds us of this identity. It reminds us that we are intimately connected, united in one Body, and as such there is nothing more important than to give ourselves to one another in love. Most of all, it reminds us that we are called to do this because God does it first, because God gave his only son to be broken and given, body and blood, for us.

These are hard truths to believe. John's Gospel tells us that when *many* of Jesus' disciples heard Jesus say they must eat his flesh and drink his blood, they said (in what is one of the great understatements of all time), "This teaching is difficult; who can accept it?" (John 6:60) and, "because of this many of his disciples turned back and no longer went about with him" (John 6:66). If these earliest followers had doubts, then how much more must we well-educated, scientifically sophisticated, late-twentieth-century and early twenty-first-century Americans find ourselves with questions. We cannot help doubting, and that is why we gather here each week. For, as one author puts it, we have come to understand "both the necessity and wonder of ritual. For ritual allows those who cannot will themselves out of the secular to perform the spiritual, as dancing allows the tongue-tied man a ceremony of love."[1] As we come to this table each week, we are not required to understand; we are simply invited to receive, to accept what is given, and to be nourished with a life that exceeds all our imaginings.

Yesterday at my ordination, as I lay prostrate on the floor, with wave upon wave of sound washing over me, feeling your prayers joined with all those holy men and women who went before us, I realized yet again that the veil between the secular and the sacred is quite thin. When our liturgies help us to see beyond that veil, we glimpse that in the midst of all our everyday anxieties and confusions a gentle grace holds us, binding us closer than we can imagine, calling us home. Though many, we are one Body. That is what we were created to be, that is why we need each other so completely.

I cannot express how grateful I am for all you have given me, all that God has given me through you. I only hope to return that gift, by letting my life be broken and given for you.

Remember and do not forget how the Lord, your God, guided you through a vast and terrible desert and fed you with bread from heaven.

CONVERSATION QUESTIONS

1. Recall a significant experience of the Eucharist. How did it nurture your own faith life?

2. The Eucharist was a matter of life and death for ancient Christians. How might the Eucharist still be a matter of life and death for us today?

3. What does it mean to be *one* body in Christ? How has the Eucharist helped you become one with the Church?

4. Parishes in different locations celebrate the Eucharist in different ways. Do you think liturgical variety is good? Why or why not?

5. Why are the actions "take, bless, break, and give" so important to the celebration of the Eucharist? What is the significance of each action?

6. In what ministries of the Eucharist have you participated? What have you gained from these experiences? In which ministries do you have a desire to participate? How might you fulfill this desire?

7. The Eucharist has been described as a many-faceted jewel because it needs to be looked at from different angles if it is going to be appreciated. What is your favorite "angle" on the Eucharist? Why does it enrich your faith so effectively?

8. The Eucharist is a sacrifice that is directly linked to the sacrifice of Jesus Christ on the cross. What makes a sacrifice meaningful? What sacrifices in your life can you unite with the sacrifice of Jesus and offer to God during the Eucharist?

9. We celebrate and receive the Eucharist in order to be able to bring "eucharist" to the world. How might you bring the presence of Jesus to others, and especially to people in need?

PART THREE

SACRAMENTS OF HEALING

✝

PENANCE

†

1422 "Those who approach the sacrament of Penance obtain pardon from God's mercy for the offense committed against him, and are, at the same time, reconciled with the Church which they have wounded by their sins and which by charity, by example, and by prayer labors for their conversion."[1]

1423 It is called the *sacrament of conversion* because it makes sacramentally present Jesus' call to conversion, the first step in returning to the Father from whom one has strayed by sin [cf. Mark 1:15; Luke 15:18].

It is called the *sacrament of Penance*, since it consecrates the Christian sinner's personal and ecclesial steps of conversion, penance, and satisfaction.

1424 It is called the *sacrament of confession*, since the disclosure or confession of sins to a priest is an essential element of this sacrament. In a profound sense it is also a "confession"— acknowledgment and praise—of the holiness of God and of his mercy toward sinful man.

It is called the *sacrament of forgiveness,* since by the priest's sacramental absolution God grants the penitent "pardon and peace."[2]

It is called the *sacrament of Reconciliation,* because it imparts to the sinner the love of God who reconciles: "Be reconciled to God" [2 Cor 5:20]. He who lives by God's merciful love is ready to respond to the Lord's call: "Go; first be reconciled to your brother" [Matt 5:24].

RITE OF PENANCE (FORM A)

RECEPTION OF THE PENITENT

When the penitent comes to confess his sins, the priest welcomes him warmly and greets him with kindness.

Then the penitent makes the sign of the cross which the priest may make also.

In the name of the Father, and of the Son, and of the
   Holy Spirit. Amen.

The priest invites the penitent to have trust in God, in these or similar words:

May God, who has enlightened every heart, help you to
   know your sins and trust in his mercy.

R. **Amen.**

READING OF THE WORD OF GOD (OPTIONAL)

Then the priest may read or say from memory a text of Scripture which proclaims God's mercy and calls man to conversion. The priest and penitent may choose other readings from Scripture.

CONFESSION OF SINS AND ACCEPTANCE OF SATISFACTION

Where it is the custom, the penitent says a general formula for confession (for example, "I confess to almighty God...") before he confesses his sins.

If necessary, the priest helps the penitent to make an integral confession and gives him suitable counsel. He urges him to be sorry for his faults, reminding him that through the sacrament of penance the Christian dies and rises with Christ and is thus renewed in the paschal mystery. The priest proposes an act of penance which the penitent accepts to make satisfaction for sin and to amend his life.

The priest should make sure that he adapts his counsel to the penitent's circumstances.

PRAYER OF THE PENITENT AND ABSOLUTION

The priest then asks the penitent to express his sorrow, which the penitent may do in these or similar words:

My God, I am sorry for my sins with all my heart. In choosing to do wrong and failing to do good, I have sinned against you whom I should love above all things. I firmly intend, with your help, to do penance, to sin no more, and to avoid whatever leads me to sin. Our Savior Jesus Christ suffered and died for us. In his name, my God, have mercy.

ABSOLUTION

Then the priest extends his hands over the penitent's head (or at least extends his right hand) and says:

God, the Father of mercies, through the death and resurrection of his Son has reconciled the world to himself and sent the Holy Spirit among us for the forgiveness of sins; through the ministry of the Church may God give you pardon and peace, and I absolve you from your sins in the name of the Father, and of the Son, + and of the Holy Spirit.

R. **Amen.**

PROCLAMATION OF PRAISE OF GOD AND DISMISSAL

After the absolution, the priest continues:

Give thanks to the Lord, for he is good.

R. **His mercy endures forever.**

May the Passion of our Lord Jesus Christ, the intercession of the Blessed Virgin Mary, and of all the saints, whatever good you do and suffering you endure, heal your sins, help you to grow in holiness, and reward you with eternal life. Go in peace.

15. Why Go to Confession?

John F. Baldovin, SJ

Many older Catholics can remember the practice in their youth of weekly confession on Saturday afternoons. There was a kind of unwritten rule that if you wanted to go to holy communion on Sunday, you needed to go to confession on Saturday. Of course, the timing minimized the likelihood that you would sin seriously before the next morning. Remember, these were the days when the weekly Mass of obligation had to be celebrated on Sunday before noon. The Saturday afternoon timing might also have favored those who ate meat on Friday. (Why was it so tempting in those days to eat meat on Friday?)

Of course, today, the situation is much changed. There are no long lines at several confessionals in the church on Saturdays. (I recall that, depending on what you had to confess, choosing between the monsignor and the two curates took some discernment—in those days all the priests would be on confession duty on a Saturday afternoon.) My usual experience as a priest helping in suburban parishes is that perhaps two or three people might come to confess in an hour and a half period. The numbers increase when a parish has a communal penance service (that is, what's normally called Rite 2 with a communal service and individual confessions), often calling on outside priests to help. Mostly, this seems to happen twice a year—in Advent and in Lent, and even then, at least in my experience, the churches are hardly full of penitents.

Many complain that the sacrament has fallen onto hard times and lament its imminent demise. Perhaps a little historical perspective might be helpful. For the Church's first thousand years, penance was an extremely serious affair and could be undertaken only once in a lifetime. In fact, for the first few centuries it wasn't all that clear that anyone who fell into serious sin (usually murder, adultery, or apostasy) *could* be forgiven their sin. There is small wonder that a number of people—some of them famous like the Emperor Constantine, who had after all killed off one wife and two sons—hedged their bets and put off baptism until their deathbed. One could avoid a lifetime as a penitent by entering a monastery, but then again, Saint Benedict said that the whole of a monk's life was a Lent! Gradually the public penitential practice was eased and people began adopting the practice of more frequent confession, even for less serious sins. Up to the twelfth century it seems that people could go to spiritual advisers, some of whom were not priests. By the thirteenth century the present requirement of an annual confession of serious sins to *one's parish priest* was in place together with the requirement of receiving holy communion during Eastertide.

Even today, one is required only to confess one's serious (or mortal) sins as completely as one can. I think it's fair to say that what's happened in the last forty years or so is that people's perception of serious sin has changed significantly. No doubt the disappearance of eating meat on Friday as well as disagreement over people's culpability in sexual matters like artificial contraception have had a great deal to do with the change in perception of what constitutes a mortal sin. It's not too much of a stretch to argue that hell has been greatly depopulated over the past forty years or so.

Now the stress on the positive aspects of our Christian faith is very good news indeed. People are much more accustomed nowadays to pay more attention to God's love, mercy, and compassion than to their sins. They recognize too—if they have been well catechized—that in order to commit a serious sin, three things are required: serious matter, knowledge by the person, and freedom of choice. I suspect it is true that people who are honestly striving to lead good Christian lives do not often commit serious sins.

What's the problem, then? Why do some lament the apparent disappearance of frequent confession? Why go to confession at all, especially if one is not conscious of serious sin? I think there are at least three answers to those questions.

The first is that we human beings have a great propensity for self-deception. Some people, of course, have the opposite problem and scrutinize their motives endlessly (sometimes to the point of an unhealthy scrupulosity), but I think that the vast majority of us are not terribly vigilant about our wrongdoing. And even when we do recognize our wrongdoing and admit it before God, we run the risk of underestimating or overestimating it. There is something very honest and human about admitting our sins before another human being, who stands as a very tangible representative of God and the Church. It is from this ordained priest that we can hear the declaration of God's pardon in a way that we can hear it from no one else. Moreover, because of the solemn seal of the confessional, this is literally the safest place on earth. I am quite sure that God does forgive our sins when we confess them honestly to him, but the genius of sacramentality is that things like forgiveness, healing, and God's self-gift all become very real for us in their being ritualized by human beings and (in the case of the other sacraments) the material goods of the earth.

The second reason for going to confession is the development of a good habit. I remember a conversation with an undergraduate a number of years ago. He was asking about confession because he was unfamiliar with it. A Catholic, he had gone to confession only once in his life—before his first holy communion at the age of eight! Presumably the situation was not dire, that is, he had committed no serious sin, but at the same time he was missing out on a valuable opportunity to take stock of his life before the Lord. It is essential for our growth in holiness that we regularly take time for a completely honest examination of conscience. It seems that today people who are involved in Twelve Step programs have a much better sense of this than the broader Catholic population. Significant events do have a big impact on our lives, but so do ordinary repetitive patterns.

The last of the (many possible) reasons for going to confession is the fact that regular confession helps us to recognize the extent of God's grace in our lives. I frequently say to penitents, "You may think this sacrament is about how bad you are, but in reality it's about how good God is." It's difficult sometimes to realize that sin is only sin when we see it in the context of God's mercy. Otherwise our misdeeds are merely wrongdoing. When we can see our wrongdoing as an offense against the God of love, we get a gut sense of what the eighteenth-century clergyman and poet John Newton meant when he wrote, "Amazing grace, how sweet the sound, that saved a wretch like me." The tangible, sacramental act of penance and reconciliation actually saves us from the wretchedness of our misdeeds. The indispensable admission ticket to Christianity is gratitude to the God who forgives us our sins so that we can live the life he wants for us.

Certainly, the sacrament of penance has taken a number of different forms over the centuries. How it will develop in the future is anyone's guess, but I am convinced it still has great value today—for anyone who needs to hear with regularity the spoken word of God's forgiving love, and that means anyone who wants to be called a Christian.

16. How to Go to Confession

Kurt Stasiak, OSB

It used to be that Catholics learned how to go to confession with their mother's milk. What to say, how to say it—and, of course, what didn't happen if you didn't say it—learning about these things was simply part of growing up Catholic. Today, though, there are many who aren't quite sure what the sacrament of reconciliation (or penance or confession) is about, much less how to go about celebrating it. The previous chapter has offered some insights on why it is important to go to confession. Here I try to clarify how one actually goes about celebrating this sacrament of God's mercy. An important first point: there is no one, precise, "exactly right" way to go to confession. God's offer of forgiveness won't grind to a halt if you're confused about what to do next or you forget the words of a certain prayer. The priest is not a referee, scrupulously vigilant that you stay "in bounds" and follow all the rules of the confessional. He is there to help you celebrate the sacrament as honestly, peacefully, and prayerfully as you can. Be reassured, your confessor does not expect or demand perfection— neither in your life, nor in the way you confess.

As you enter the confessional (or reconciliation chapel), it is your choice to confess face to face or behind the screen. In either instance, the priest may offer a greeting such as "Peace be with you," or he may recite a brief passage from the Bible. Some priests may simply wait for you to begin. (Again, there is no one way to celebrate the sacrament.) After the greeting or reading, or if it seems the priest wants you to take the lead, make the sign of the cross and then say how long it has been since your last confession. (If you can't remember exactly when that was, tell the priest that or make an educated guess.)

Who are you? The priest doesn't need to know your name, but it can be helpful if he has at least a general idea of who you are and what you do. For example, "Father, it's been six weeks or so since I last came to confession. I'm in my thirties, am married, and have two kids." Or, "It's been about three months. I'm a sophomore in college." Or, "I'm in my twenties, Father. My last confession was just before Christmas. I'm getting married soon, and my fiancée and I want to start things off right." These brief comments don't relate your life history, of course, but they do provide the priest with a context that may help him better understand your confession.

What to confess? Many prayer books offer various forms of an examination of conscience. No matter which particular form you choose, as you examine your conscience—ideally a few hours, or even a day or two before your confession—the basic questions are the following: What are my responsibilities (as spouse, parent, child, employer, worker, friend, and so forth)? How am I, or am I not, living out those responsibilities?

Our Church requires us to confess any mortal (grave or serious) sins we have committed, as well as revealing how often we have fallen. The point here is not that the priest is keeping score (he isn't), but the better your confessor understands how often you struggle with your sins, the better position he is in to offer you counsel or advice.

While we aren't required to confess venial (ordinary or "daily") sins, it is often worth our while to do so. Bringing these ordinary faults and weaknesses to the sacrament helps us work on our conversion and grow in God's grace a little more each day.

How to confess? Sins don't have to be confessed in any particular order or in any particular way. Here is an example of how two men, each in his forties, each married with children, confess essentially the same sins but in a manner unique to each:

> *Peter*: I sinned against the third commandment [You shall keep holy the Lord's Day] once. I used the Lord's name in vain probably several times a week. I committed some sins in thought against the ninth commandment [You shall not covet your neighbor's wife] a few times. I did tell a couple of lies, mostly harmless. I committed a venial sin against the fifth commandment [You shall not kill] when I drank a little too much at a party. For these and all the sins of my past life, I am truly sorry.

> *Paul*: Father, the thing that bothers me the most is that I don't always give my kids the kind of example I want to give them. My language isn't always the best. I know that they know I fudge a little on the truth, sometimes. Two things, in particular. I came home from a party last Saturday just a little bit woozy. Had a little too much to drink. Two of my kids saw that, and I wish they hadn't. I made it even worse the next day, because I was really wiped out and just didn't bother to get up for Sunday Mass. Also, although they don't know this, of course, I still have impure thoughts and desires at times. Most of all, I'd just like to be a better dad to my children. I think that is all, Father. I ask for your forgiveness.

Notice that the sins Peter and Paul confess are pretty much the same. *How* they confess those sins, however, differs. Peter follows a traditional examination of conscience based upon the

Ten Commandments. Paul uses his desire to be a good father as a reference point from which to focus his confession. Are both confessions *good*? Yes. Are both confessions *right*? Yes. Both Peter and Paul have confessed in a satisfactory and appropriate way. The point of this example is not to assign a "higher grade" to one confession, but rather to illustrate the different ways in which sins can be confessed.

After you have confessed, the priest may offer you some words of advice or encouragement. Sometimes people are concerned about the questions the priest might ask. Be assured that if the priest does ask a question, it is because he believes he needs to know something more about what you have said in order to minister more effectively and more directly to you. And certainly you may ask the priest any questions you have, either to better understand something he has said or to ask about something that concerns you. The priest will then give you a penance and ask you to make an act of contrition.

Act of contrition and absolution. Your act of contrition may be in your own words, or you may take it from a book. It can be as succinct as, "Lord Jesus, Son of God, have mercy on me, a sinner," or it may take a longer form, such as the following:

> *My God, I am sorry for my sins*
> *with all my heart. In choosing to*
> *do wrong and failing to do good,*
> *I have sinned against you whom*
> *I should love above all things. I*
> *firmly intend, with your help, to*
> *do penance, to sin no more, and*
> *to avoid whatever leads me to sin.*
> *Our Savior Jesus Christ suffered*
> *and died for us. In his name, my*
> *God, have mercy.*

The priest will now say the words of absolution—the prayerful assurance that God, who welcomes the repentant sinner, forgives your sins. It is interesting to note that before the Second Vatican Council the priest would say the words of absolution in Latin while the penitent was making his or her act of contrition. The words of absolution are now said in English, and they follow your act of contrition, so you can hear these words of mercy and peace!

Let us conclude. After pronouncing absolution, the priest will say something along the lines of "Go in peace" or "God bless you." You may respond with "Thanks be to God" or even a simple "Thank you, Father." This concludes the *celebration* of the sacrament, but of course there is still something to be done: your penance.

If the priest has given you prayers as your penance, you may say those before you leave the church or at a better, more appropriate, time. And, whether your act of penance is prayers that can be said right away or actions to be performed later, it is good to spend at least a few moments in church thinking about what you have just done—and about what God has done for you: forgiveness, pardon, and peace. Good reasons to linger in the church for a while and give God thanks!

In conclusion, the sacrament of reconciliation is meant to ease our burdens, not increase them. The confessional is a place where we sacramentally encounter God's mercy, not a stage upon which memorized lines must be recited perfectly. There is no one perfect way to go to confession. After all, the sacrament is a gift precisely for people who are imperfect! And remember that the priest is there as a helper and guide. He is there, as the *Catechism* says, "not [as] the master of God's forgiveness, but [as] its servant."

CONVERSATION QUESTIONS

1. Which of the names listed by the *Catechism* (1423–24) do you prefer for this sacrament? Why?

2. We often think of conversion as a single event that happened in the past (e.g., when someone converts to Christianity). However, the sacrament of penance is also rightly called a sacrament of conversion. How might it be a sacrament of conversion in your life?

3. What is sin? How does the way you define sin affect the way you see the sacrament of penance?

4. What roles do guilt and anxiety play in today's society and in your own life? How might the sacrament of penance help to alleviate guilt and anxiety?

5. When we have harmed others, being truly forgiven by friends and family is usually a wonderful experience. Why, then, do you think so few people celebrate the sacrament of reconciliation?

6. What is the purpose of doing penance? If we are already forgiven by God, why should we want to do penance?

7. How might you celebrate this sacrament more regularly in your own faith life? Encourage others to do so?

ANOINTING
OF THE SICK

✝

1511 The Church believes and confesses that among the seven sacraments there is one especially intended to strengthen those who are being tried by illness, the Anointing of the Sick:

> This sacred anointing of the sick was instituted by Christ our Lord as a true and proper sacrament of the New Testament. It is alluded to indeed by Mark, but is recommended to the faithful and promulgated by James the apostle and brother of the Lord.[1]

1503 Christ's compassion toward the sick and his many healings of every kind of infirmity are a resplendent sign that "God has visited his people" [Luke 7:16; cf. Matt 4:24] and that the Kingdom of God is close at hand. Jesus has the power not only to heal, but also to forgive sins [cf. Mark 2:5–12]; he has come to heal the whole man, soul and body; he is the physician the sick have need of [cf. Mark 2:17]. His compassion toward all who suffer goes so far that he identifies himself with them: "I was sick and you visited me" [Matt 25:36]. His preferential love for the sick has not ceased through the centuries to draw the very special attention of Christians toward all those who suffer in body and soul. It is the source of tireless efforts to comfort them.

ANOINTING OF THE SICK OUTSIDE OF MASS

PRAYER OVER THE OIL

When the priest blesses the oil during the rite, he uses the following blessing:

God of all consolation,
you chose and sent your Son to heal the world.
Graciously listen to our prayer of faith:
send the power of the Holy Spirit, the Consoler,
into this precious oil, this soothing ointment,
this rich gift, this fruit of the earth.
Bless this oil + and sanctify it for our use.
Make this oil a remedy for all who are anointed
with it;
heal them in body, in soul, and in spirit,
and deliver them from every affliction.
We ask this through our Lord Jesus Christ, your Son,
who lives and reigns with you and the Holy Spirit,
one God, for ever and ever.

R. **Amen.**

The priest anoints the sick person with blessed oil.
First, he anoints the forehead, saying:

Through this holy anointing
may the Lord in his love and mercy
help you with the grace of the Holy Spirit.

R. **Amen.**

Then he anoints the hands, saying:

May the Lord who frees you from sin
save you and raise you up.

R. **Amen.**

PRAYER AFTER ANOINTING

The priest says a prayer. One of the prayers is as follows:
Let us pray.

Father in heaven,
through this holy anointing
grant N. comfort in his/her suffering.
When he/she is afraid, give him/her courage,
when afflicted, give him/her patience,
when dejected, afford him/her hope,
and when alone, assure him/her of the support of
    your holy people.
We ask this through Christ our Lord.

R. **Amen.**

17. The Richness of Tradition

Lizette Larson-Miller

Caring for the sick and dying is a basic human act of charity and justice; it is not limited to Christians. But when Christians engage in care for the sick, they do so in imitation of Christ's compassion and action.

In light of the centrality of Jesus' own healing ministry, it is not surprising that we possess many writings from Church history that commend healing ministry and give instructions for what to say and do in private prayer and liturgy. But just as our knowledge of the history of all the sacraments has greatly expanded in the past hundred years, so has our knowledge of the richness of the tradition of how the Church has cared for its sick and dying members. We know that the trajectory through history is not a single thread, but one of tremendous variety in the earliest centuries that grows into uniformity in some geographical areas. In this overview of the history of the sacrament of the anointing of the sick, we divide Western (or primarily Latin-speaking) Church history—the ancestry of contemporary Roman Catholic practice—into three broad periods: early Church/medieval, late medieval/Middle Ages, and contemporary. We do so in order to more easily trace changes and returns in our history.

Early Church/medieval: Throughout the first six centuries of the Christian era, we find our forebears in the faith relying heavily on two New Testament passages regarding ritual care for the sick:

> [The apostles] went out and proclaimed that all should repent. They cast out many demons, and anointed with oil many who were sick and cured them. (Mark 6:12–13)

> Are any among you sick? They should call for the elders of the church and have them pray over them, anointing them with oil in the name of the Lord. The prayer of faith will save the sick, and the Lord will raise them up; and anyone who has committed sins will be forgiven. (Jas 5:14–15)

Both of these passages describe the actions of the followers of Jesus as prayer (in one case, exorcistic prayer), touch, and anointing with oil, and the results—the effects of these ecclesial actions—were healing of mind and body and spirit in the curing of the body and forgiveness of sins. We learn from various church orders (books describing how to do church) that in some places the bishop was the normative minister of healing; in other places that role was done by priests and deacons; and in still other places the primary ecclesial identity of healing was in the oil itself, blessed by the bishop, which allowed any baptized Christian to do the anointing.

As Christianity spread out of urban areas and north of the Alps into what was known as Gaul, fifth-century and later pastoral care of the sick took on a multiplicity of ritual expressions. We know that while episcopally blessed oil, prayer, and laying on of hands were primary ways the Church ministered to the sick, there were other practices: the giving of blessed bread, the drinking of holy water, incubation (spending the night in sleep and dreams at martyr shrines), and the "making" of holy oil by running oil through the tombs of martyrs. All were understood as part of the Church's healing ministry, complementing the sacramental ministry centered on anointing with oil. Note that this holistic anointing for physical, mental, emotional, and spiritual healing was not the sacrament of the dying. The sacrament for the dying was the last communion, or *viaticum*, already an "old and canonical law still to be observed" at the time of the Council of Nicaea in 325. This ancient tradition remained a constant, along with rituals of prayer, the chanting of the gospel passions, and psalms, to accompany the "migration of the soul" to the holy city of Jerusalem.

In the medieval church, beginning about the eighth century in what is now Europe and the Mediterranean world, the Church's rituals for the sick still centered on prayer, the laying on of hands, and anointing, but the interpretation of the effects of those rituals, along with the understanding of the human person—Christian anthropology—was rapidly changing, affecting the sacramental form (words) and timing of the actions. The Church found itself needing to adapt to different cultures and philosophical systems. One cultural aspect that the Roman Church met was the association of anointing with a change in status. The baptismal anointing changed one's status—one became a member of the Church, part of the Body of Christ, fit for heaven. In Frankish culture and in other European tribal communities, kings and other hereditary leaders were also anointed, and so their status changed—they were now royalty. How did the anointing of the sick, with its formula changed to match a baptismal chrismation and a royal anointing, "I anoint you with holy oil as Samuel anointed David," change their status? It often meant that recovering from an illness after anointing would have a lifelong effect on the survivor.

Just as the sacrament for the dying was needed, as mentioned above in the early Church description, here a mention of the sacrament of reconciliation or confession is necessary. In the early Church sins were forgiven through baptism, through prayer, through mutual forgiveness (one Christian to another), through participation in the Eucharist, or for serious sins (such as adultery, murder, or apostasy), through public or canonical penance. This was a three-to-seven-year process by which the excommunicated sinner was "re-formed" through penance, fasting, prayer, and the prayers of the community; gradually readmitted to the community; and reconciled by the reception of communion. And, most important, this could be done only once in a person's post-baptismal life. In the seventh through ninth centuries another pattern emerged in which the monastic practices of Celtic churches gave rise to an individual and repeatable spiritual direction that included confession, an assignment of practices to rectify the situation, and a blessing. This gradually shifted to the confessor being ordained (most monks were not), and a reversal of penance and blessing, so that the blessing, or absolution, was given before the penance was fulfilled. This individualized confession became far more popular than public penance, even though the latter was still official until 1215. Between the eighth and thirteenth centuries this repeatable confession for the forgiveness of sins became intertwined with the anointing of the sick because the anointing of the sick was focusing more on spiritual sickness than on physical sickness. The holistic healing of the early Church was increasingly seen as less important than the illness and healing of the soul, which was healed through absolution. Furthermore, the shift to only a priest being capable of offering absolution would result in a logical extension of that same restriction to anointing the sick.

The Middle Ages: The pattern of three sequential rites for the seriously sick—confession, anointing, and *viaticum*—resulted in another theological conversation among university scholars in the eleventh through thirteenth centuries. These "schoolmen" or Scholastics, tried to distinguish the different types of sin that these three sacraments forgave. They also saw an important balance in the Christian life as it was lived between the first anointing at baptism and the final anointing at death. These conversations on the various types of sin and the first and last anointings led to a change in the order of sacraments that made sense to the pastoral needs of the dying: confession, *viaticum*, and the last anointing, *unctionis extremis*, especially as the last, or extreme, anointing was linked to the changing of status from this life to eternal life.

Reformations: From the fifteenth through the seventeenth centuries the Western church was challenged by a series of reformations—all hoping to correct practices that were believed to have obscured the truth of the early Church. The Council of Trent, in two different sessions, addressed the challenges of Protestant reformations by defending extreme unction as one of seven sacraments instituted by Christ (DS 1601), and as a reforming council, also argued that the anointing was not just for those about to die but for those who were seriously sick (Council of Trent, Session 7). In the antagonistic conversations of the time, however, the reforming aspects of the Council of Trent were lost, and the practice continued as an anointing for death at the end of the "last rites."

We also need to remember that while the anointing was commonly for dying, other ecclesial activities were retained or enlivened for healing: the rise of pilgrimages from the ninth century on, later healing shrines such as Lourdes were expanded, and popular practices such as novenas, prayers, votive masses, and patron saints expanded the repertoire of Catholic healing, along with the visitation and care for the sick by individual Christians and religious orders, which had always been present throughout Christian history.

Contemporary: The post–Vatican II rites for the sick and dying, contained in *The Pastoral Care of the Sick*, reflect elements from each of these broad periods of history. But like all liturgical and sacramental reforms, the historical development is essential to understanding: "History is a science not of past happenings, but of present understanding."[1] A sacramental formula of the anointing of the sick invites us to hear again the words of the Letter of Saint James, but not as a slavish reconstruction of ancient practice.

The placement of the sacrament of anointing in the midst of a whole variety of rituals and prayers to be led by the priesthood of all believers honors the variety and richness of different practices of healing through the centuries. And the clarity of the sacrament of the dying, *viaticum*, is restored but continues to be nuanced in light of how people actually die in the twenty-first century. Something old and always new, "this sacrament gives the grace of the Holy Spirit to those who are sick: by this grace the whole person is healed and saved, sustained by trust in God, and strengthened against the temptations of the Evil One and against anxiety over death."[2]

18. Anointing as Pastoral Sacrament

Bruce T. Morrill, SJ

The renewal of the anointing of the sick in the Catholic Church is an ongoing effort to rescue the sacrament from its own malaise as "extreme unction," a medieval and post-Tridentine practiced theology that has proven quite virulent in its resistance to the reform prescribed by Vatican II. The postconciliar rite replaces the mechanistic view of anointing as cleansing the soul for immediate entry into the beatific vision (and, thus, the priest's bedside arrival as a veritable declaration of death), with a symbolic meaning and purpose far more resonant with the faith revealed in the gospel. The latter redefines the sacrament as one of healing, the recognition that God is working through human symbolism as part of a larger sacramental reality of shared faith within a community of believers. Bracketing the isolated, condensed manner of anointing the sick in emergencies as an abbreviated rite necessitated "by the special circumstances of hospital ministry,"[1] the reformed rite envisions the sacrament's typical celebration as part of a larger process of pastoral care for the sick and elderly. The ways divine grace becomes real in pastoral practice of this sacrament comes through the uniqueness of each human story. The following story comes from my own pastoral work as an exemplary case for understanding the theology of this beautiful rite.

***

Since the year 2000 I have been occasionally serving Yup'ik Eskimo villages in the Hooper Bay region on the Bering Seacoast of Alaska, making the long trip from Boston either at Easter or Christmas time as my academic schedule allows. In the early 1980s, after finishing college, I had spent a year as a Jesuit volunteer in a village further north at the mouth of the Yukon River. Twenty years later I was surprised yet consoled to discern a call once again to be of pastoral service to those villages. I have made seven trips since then, most for about ten days, although I spent seven weeks in one village in the summer of 2001. I have come to forge close ties with folks of all ages in that village of about seven hundred people.

The settlement sits on a high spot of tundra overlooking serpentine sloughs, whipped by Bering winds, the people practicing subsistence living while constantly teetering on the edge of poverty, steeped in their native traditions yet caught between that primordial world and the relentlessly encroaching culture of media-driven consumption. One of the enduring Yup'ik values, nevertheless, is reverence and care for elders. This story is about one such elder, an eighty-year-old woman whom I shall call Mary.

My most recent trip to that particular village, for Holy Week and Easter, was my first extended stay there in a few years, having made only a one-night visit during Christmas two years before. I had, however, kept in touch with a couple of leading figures in the parish, one of whom had apprised me of a number of deaths that had occurred over the past year. The day before Palm Sunday I landed in the village, word of my arrival circulated, and I celebrated Mass with about a dozen people in the early evening. Before starting, I inquired about the families of those who had died, as well as the condition of certain elders, especially Mary. I already knew that two of the recently deceased were Mary's brother and sister, but I was shocked to learn that another was one of her daughters, Sarah, a single parent in her forties who had succumbed to cancer. Yes, advised the leader of the parish's

119

eucharistic ministers, who faithfully bring holy communion to the homebound, Mary was still in her home and able to receive guests, and yes, she would especially benefit from a pastoral visit. After Mass, I took a pyx containing a few hosts and a copy of the *The Pastoral Care of the Sick* and walked the short distance to Mary's house.

Typical of homes in the Yup'ik villages, four generations live under Mary's roof, a crowded, hard-worn, prefabricated structure with a kitchen and living area in the center and small pairs of bedrooms on each end. That evening I entered a scene of all ages in the common room: Mary's fifty-something son, Paul, a widower, preparing dinner with his daughter; the daughter's toddler playing on the floor; Paul's niece and another teenaged girl eating at the table; a brother watching television; and finally, Mary, occupying a minuscule portion of the couch. She had clearly aged over the past couple of years, shortened by osteoporosis (Paul later commented, "My Mom keeps shrinking!"), thinner, hearing and sight somewhat diminished, but still able to get around with a walker. I received greetings all around, but Mary did not recognize me at first (truth is, I had aged a fair amount over the past couple of years, as well), so Paul showed her a five-year-old photo of me on the wall, which sparked the connection. She smiled and clasped my hand in a still forceful grip, repeatedly saying "thank you" in Yup'ik.

Like many of the elders, including her late husband, James, Mary had never learned English. Mary made her way to the table and, very much the matriarch, instructed her son and granddaughter to serve me supper. As we all ate together, with Paul translating between his mother and myself, our conversation slowly shifted to the heavy stories of recent deaths. The story of Mary's elder sister's death included some remarkable occurrences in weather that served as signs of consolation to the family, contrasting with the account of her daughter's succumbing to cancer, remaining quietly at home, no doubt in much pain, to the end. During the conversation the younger people had gradually drifted into other rooms. As I noticed the grief written on Mary's face, Paul said that his mother wanted to talk more about this. Mary was pondering two things: How was she to pray during this coming Holy Week? Why was God keeping her on this earth, while her daughter, brother, sister, and, three years earlier, her husband had all been taken, leaving her behind? I knew it was not a moment for abstract explanations but, rather, a story. I was profoundly grateful to have a good one to share with Mary.

I asked Mary to remember the time we had first met during my initial pastoral stay in the village six-and-a-half years earlier. The Jesuit who serves the region, in explaining his routine for the daily evening Mass, noted that after Mass each night he regularly brought communion to one elderly couple who used to attend faithfully but were now homebound. I accompanied him to James and Mary's home my first night there, and after he departed the next day for other villages, I made a point of doing so daily for the duration of my stay. Mary was frail (hobbled by an old, untreated foot and leg injury), but her mind was sharp, while James, some ten years her senior, lived with significant bodily and communicative debilitation due to a stroke. Their material poverty, the crowded quarters housing several generations, the elders' inability to speak English, the complete care the younger generations gave them (including serving as translators)—none of these things surprised me much, given my year's stay in a similar village nearly two decades earlier. What impressed me deeply, however, was the profound reverence, the palpable *joy*, the consoling humility with which this aged couple celebrated the service of holy communion. They had long ago memorized the English responses to the parts of the Mass, many of which function in the communion service as well. After the brief reading from Scripture and my beginning the Prayers of the Faithful, Mary would offer in Yup'ik extended prayers of intercession, followed by the couple and as many family as had gathered around reciting the Lord's Prayer in their native language. I would then administer holy communion to the couple and Sarah, who was primarily caring for them, and perhaps some others, after which followed silent prayer, the blessing, and then a greeting of peace shared by every person in the house, regardless of whether he or she had joined in the service.

My primary pastoral role was simply to lead them prayerfully in the rite as found in the *The Pastoral Care of the Sick*, doing what the Church does, a shared practice of the tradition that both served the faith of the elderly Yup'ik couple and quickly bonded us all. I was present in a posture of service to the elders, but the enacted ritual worship was affecting the family and also transforming me. At the center of the ritual were Mary and James, whose faces and bodies proclaimed such quietly joyful faith in receiving and sharing the body of Christ, a sacramental action I came to realize was integral to the life they shared with each other and the entire family. I began to look forward to visiting them each evening. Their home was a short distance from the church, made surprisingly long that year by relentless gale winds blowing horizontal sheets of snow and rain that glazed the surface of the terrain. With jolting gusts intermittently intensifying the headwinds, I repeatedly found myself temporarily immobilized, struggling to retain my balance on stretches of glare ice, even pushed backward at times. On successive evenings as I skidded, strained, or came to a complete halt alone in the darkness, the wind howling in my ears, I would find myself marveling: What in the world am I doing here? The answer became clear in the repetition: This is the life of the gospel, and true to form, Christ is proving to be the one who has already gone ahead, waiting to meet me amid people profoundly aware of their need for God. That need—their poverty in spirit, their trust—was eliciting a desire within me to be with Christ—and thus them—that I could never have come up with on my own.

A couple of days before Christmas, Paul called to say his mother wanted me to come for lunch with her, James, and a couple of their other sons. I arrived in the brightness of noontime to find one of the daughters-in-law preparing the meal, with Mary advising. The event, I slowly came to realize, was not only an act of hospitality on the cusp of Christmas, but also a modeling of roles and practices from James and Mary to the generation succeeding them. At one point Paul recounted how his father, James, had patiently taught his sons through stories and the example of his own life. I decided to say something then to Mary and James, through Paul's translation, that had been building up in me: how over the past week they had become for me great teachers and examples of what it is to practice faith in the eucharistic Christ, how their celebration of holy communion challenged and inspired my faith. With tears in her eyes, Mary replied that all her life, since her youth at the old regional mission school, she had always thought of the priests and sisters as the people she had to learn from. She never imagined she would hear one of them calling her his teacher. I just nodded and smiled.

That was the story, abridged and focused on the witness of her faith to me, that I told Mary in response to the directionless grief and loneliness she was now experiencing, years later, in the deep wake of her recent losses and the ebb tide of her own declining physical condition. I suggested that while God's wisdom and timing are ultimately inscrutable, it seemed clear that Mary still had a role to play in this world, in her family, in the wider village and parish community who came to visit her or remembered her in their prayers. Mary's vocation, I told her, remains that of an elder to us, an example of practiced faith as an all-encompassing way of life, a source of encouragement and consolation to many through her embodiment of a world of memories and present affection. Her eyes registering acceptance, Mary responded through a serene smile with a repeated "thank you" in Yup'ik.

After a quiet moment I noted how late the hour was and that we had not yet shared holy communion. Mary asked that I first celebrate with her the sacrament of penance, which we did in one of the back rooms, and then many of the family gathered around for the communion service. In departing, I asked Paul how long it had been since Mary had received the sacrament of the anointing of the sick. He explained that she had twice been flown to the regional hospital for health crises during the past couple of years and most likely had been anointed at some point. I averred that the present seemed like a beneficial moment for her to celebrate the sacrament again, if she were to understand it not as last rites but as an anointing to strengthen and support her in her weakened condition and new spiritual challenges. Paul immediately nodded that he knew what I meant, saying they had been catechized in the reformed theology and practice of the sacrament. Paul later conferred with Mary, and we looked forward to celebrating the sacrament of anointing with her at some point in Holy Week.

CONVERSATION QUESTIONS

1. The anointing of the sick can be considered an anointing to strengthen and support them in their weakened condition and new spiritual challenges. What does it mean to be healthy? How do we judge who is healthy and who is sick?

2. What role should the faith community play in the celebration of the anointing of the sick? Is it better for a community to be present during this sacrament?

3. Why do you think touch is so important in the process of healing? Thinking of times when you have been sick or caring for someone who is sick, how has touch helped alleviate suffering?

4. What are some ways that your parish might encourage the celebration of this sacrament? What are some ways that you might participate more actively in Jesus' healing ministry?

5. Is there a healing needed in your own life at this time (physical, spiritual, or relational)? Will you pray for the grace you need?

PART FOUR

Sacraments of Vocation

✝

MARRIAGE

✝

1601 "The matrimonial covenant, by which a man and a woman establish between themselves a partnership of the whole of life, is by its nature ordered toward the good of the spouses and the procreation and education of offspring; this covenant between baptized persons has been raised by Christ the Lord to the dignity of a sacrament."[1]

1613 On the threshold of his public life Jesus performs his first sign—at his mother's request—during a wedding feast [cf. John 2:1–11]. The Church attaches great importance to Jesus' presence at the wedding at Cana. She sees in it the confirmation of the goodness of marriage and the proclamation that thenceforth marriage will be an efficacious sign of Christ's presence.

1621 In the Latin Rite the celebration of marriage between two Catholic faithful normally takes place during Holy Mass, because of the connection of all the sacraments with the Paschal mystery of Christ.[2] In the Eucharist the memorial of the New Covenant is realized, the New Covenant in which Christ has united himself for ever to the Church, his beloved bride for whom he gave himself up.[3] It is therefore fitting that the spouses should seal their consent to give themselves to each other through the offering of their own lives by uniting it to the offering of Christ for his Church made present in the Eucharistic sacrifice, and by receiving the Eucharist so that, communicating in the same Body and the same Blood of Christ, they may form but "one body" in Christ [cf. 1 Cor 10:17].

NUPTIAL BLESSING (FORM C)

The Priest, with hands joined, calls upon those present to pray, saying:

> Let us humbly invoke by our prayers, dear brothers and
> sisters,
> God's blessings upon this bride and groom,
> that in his kindness he may favor with his help
> those on whom he has bestowed the Sacrament of
> Matrimony.

All pray in silence. Then the Priest, with hands extended over the bride and bridegroom continues:

> Holy Father, maker of the whole world,
> who created man and woman in your own image
> and willed that their union be crowned with your
> blessing,
> we humbly beseech you for these your servants,
> who are joined today in the Sacrament of Matrimony.

> May your abundant blessing, Lord,
> come down upon this bride, N.,
> and upon N., her companion for life,
> and may the power of your Holy Spirit

set their hearts aflame from on high,
so that, living out together the gift of Matrimony,
they may (adorn their family with children and)
enrich the Church.

In happiness may they praise you, O Lord,
in sorrow may they seek you out;
may they have the joy of your presence
to assist them in their toil,
and know that you are near
to comfort them in their need;
let them pray to you in the holy assembly
and bear witness to you in the world,
and after a happy old age,
together with the circle of friends that surrounds
    them,
may they come to the Kingdom of Heaven.
Through Christ our Lord.

R. **Amen.**

19. The Sacrament of Marriage

MICHAEL G. LAWLER AND WILLIAM P. ROBERTS

In the Bible there is an action called a prophetic symbol. Jeremiah, for instance, buys a potter's earthen flask, dashes it to the ground before a startled crowd, and proclaims the meaning of his action. "Thus says the Lord of hosts: So will I break this people and this city, as one breaks a potter's vessel" (19:11). Ezekiel takes a brick, draws a city on it, builds siege works around the city, and lays siege to it. This city, he explains, is "Jerusalem" (4:1) and his action "a sign for the house of Israel" (4:3). He takes a sword, shaves his hair with it, and divides the hair into three bundles. One bundle he burns, another he scatters to the wind, a third he carries around Jerusalem, shredding into even smaller pieces, explaining his action in the proclamation: "This is Jerusalem" (5:5).

Self-understanding in Israel was rooted in the great covenant between the god, Yahweh, and the people, Israel. It is easy to predict that Israelites, prone to prophetic action, would search for such an action to symbolize their covenant relationship with Yahweh. It is just as easy, perhaps, to predict that the symbol they would choose is the covenant that is marriage between a man and a woman. The prophet Hosea was the first to speak of marriage as prophetic symbol of the covenant.

On a superficial level, the marriage of Hosea to his wife, Gomer, is like many other marriages. But on a level beyond the superficial, Hosea interpreted it as a prophetic symbol, proclaiming,

132

making humanly explicit, and celebrating in representation the covenant communion between Yahweh and Israel. As Gomer left Hosea for other lovers, so too did Israel leave Yahweh for other gods. As Hosea waits in faithfulness for Gomer's return, as he receives her back without recrimination, so too does Yahweh wait for and take back Israel. Hosea's human action and reaction are a prophetic symbol of Yahweh's divine action and reaction. In both covenants, the human and the divine, the covenant relationship has been violated, and Hosea's actions both mirror and reflect Yahweh's. In symbolic representation they proclaim, reveal, and celebrate not only Hosea's faithfulness to Gomer, but also Yahweh's faithfulness to Israel.

The meanings of this marriage parable, of course, are not limited to meanings for the spouses; there are also meanings for their marriage. One such meaning is this: not only is marriage a human institution, but it is also a religious, prophetic symbol, pro-claiming, revealing, and celebrating in the human world the com-munion between God and God's people. Not only is marriage a reality of social law, but it is also a reality of grace. Lived into as grace, lived into in faith, as we might say today, marriage appears as a two-tiered reality. On one tier, it bespeaks the mutual covenanted love of this man and this woman, of Hosea and Gomer; on another, it prophetically symbolizes the mutually covenanted love of God and God's people. This two-tiered view of marriage became the Christian view, articulated later in the Letter to the Ephesians (5:21–33). Jewish prophetic symbol became in history Christian sacrament.

The classical Roman Catholic definition of sacrament, "an outward sign of inward grace instituted by Christ," which took a thousand years to become established, can now be more fully explicated. A sacrament is a prophetic symbol in and through which the Church, the Body of Christ, proclaims, reveals, and celebrates in representation that presence and action of God that is called grace. To say that a marriage between Christians is a sacrament is to say, then, that it is a prophetic symbol, a two-tiered reality. On one tier, it proclaims, reveals, and celebrates the intimate communion of life and love between a man and a woman. On another, more profound tier, it proclaims, makes explicit, and celebrates the intimate communion of life and love and grace between God and God's people and between Christ and Christ's people, the Church.

Those entering marriage say to one another, before the society in which they live, "I love you and I give myself to and for you." Christians entering a specifically sacramental marriage say that too, but they also say more. They say, "I love you as Christ loves his Church, steadfastly and faithfully." From the first, therefore, a Christian marriage is intentionally more than just the communion for the whole of life of this man and this woman. It is more than just human covenant; it is also religious covenant. It is more than law and obligations and rights; it is also grace. From the first, God and God's Christ are present as third partners in it, modeling it, gracing it, and guaranteeing it. This presence of grace in its most ancient and solemn Christian sense, namely, the presence of the gracious God, is not something extrinsic to Christian marriage. It is something essential to it, something without which it would not be Christian marriage at all. Christian, sacramental marriage certainly proclaims the love of man and woman. It also proclaims, reveals, and celebrates the love of their God for God's people and of their Christ for his Church. It is in this sense that it is a sacrament, a prophetic symbol, both a sign and an instrument, of the explicit and gracious presence of Christ and of the God he reveals.

In a truly Christian marriage, which is a marriage between two believing Christians, the symbolic meaning takes precedence over the foundational meaning in the sense that the steadfast love of God and of Christ is explicitly present as the model for the love of the spouses. In and through their love, God and God's Christ are present in a Christian marriage, gracing the spouses with their presence and providing for them models of steadfast love.

There is one, final question. When the Catholic Church claims that *marriage* between baptized Christians is a sacrament, what precisely is the meaning of the word *marriage*? In ordinary language, the word is ambiguous. Sometimes it refers to the wedding ceremony, in which two people freely commit to one another "for the purpose of establishing a marriage" (can. 1057, 2). Sometimes it means, more crucially, the marriage and the life that flows from their wedding commitment, the communion of life and love that lasts until death. Both these common meanings of the word *marriage* are intended in the claim that marriage is a sacrament.

This chapter is about four interrelated personal realities: friendship, love, marriage, and the sacrament of marriage. First, there is truth in Aristotle's ancient claim that human life is impossible without friends—trusted others who understand and accept me as I am, who challenge my potential, and who rejoice with me when I attain it and console me when I don't. Friends wish me well, that is, they love me, and I love them. We share our thoughts, our feelings, our dreams, and on occasion, because we wish to be best friends for life, we marry. Second, marriage is an intimate partnership of love for the whole of life, equally ordered to the mutual well-being of the spouses and to the generation and nurture of children. Finally, when marriage is between believing Christians, it is also a sacrament, a prophetic symbol of the presence in the world of the gracious God. Every marriage between Christian believers offers, therefore, two levels of meaning. There is a first, foundational level, the communion of the whole of life between the spouses, and built on this foundation and bound to it, there is a second, symbolic level on which the communion between the spouses images and represents the communion between Christ and his Church.

20. A Promised Lifetime

COLLEEN CAMPION

During my high school years I held a part-time job at our parish rectory, answering the telephone and the doorbell each weekend. Quite often I opened the door to welcome engaged couples who came to discuss their wedding with one of the parish priests. On a table near the front door rested a stack of informational materials, including one entitled, "A Wedding Is a Day, A Marriage Is a Lifetime." The catchy title captured my attention, as it was able in a concise manner to urge couples to place as much attention on preparing for their marriage as they do in planning the wedding. In the course of my years in Catholic high school, we had certainly learned about the sacrament of matrimony and understood it to be a lifetime commitment. Each year we had observed Vocation Awareness Week, when we discerned what our own vocational call from God would be. Although marriage was always included in the discussion, the week concentrated heavily on understanding and promoting vocations to the priesthood and religious life. My classmates and I always came away feeling that, while marriage was addressed as a sacrament, the clear path to holiness seemed to be through ordination or religious consecration.

In my first year of college, at a venerable Jesuit institution, I met my husband. We dated through college, and attending the 10:00 p.m. Sunday Mass together was a hallmark of our courtship. Just after college we became engaged. As we began to plan our wedding, I could not help but remember that wedding pamphlet in the rectory office all those years before. We were thrilled in thinking about our wedding day, but we were mindful that careful preparation would also help us build a marriage that would last a lifetime. Our pre-Cana preparation program helped us broaden and deepen our understanding of marriage, enabling us to embrace the role of marriage as sacrament and vocation, intimately linked to our baptism, and ultimately, our path to holiness. Marriage, like baptism, is not a sacrament that "happens" on just the day of the ceremony. Marriage, like baptism, has to be lived out over a lifetime.

Reflecting over twenty-six years, I see that we have tried to live our marriage as a sacrament in innumerable ways, both big and small. When we were first married, my husband was in medical school and residency with a demanding and sometimes grueling on-call schedule. To support him in his needs, I took on many of the household tasks so that he could sleep and study. Now, many years later, our roles have reversed, as my husband supports me in my effort to complete a degree in pastoral ministry while working in a parish. In our support of one another in our career needs, we have each enabled one another to be Christ to the people we serve—him to his patients and me to our parishioners.

Much of our ability to deal with the bigger questions of life stemmed from some basic decisions that seemed small and insignificant at the time. One weekend early in our marriage, when our schedules had been particularly demanding, we were considering what to do for Mass. Tired and overworked, we both contemplated just sleeping that morning. For the first time in our adult lives we faced the question of why we should or should not go to Mass, accountable to no one else for that decision other than ourselves and God. We did go to Mass. We knew that in our demanding week's schedule, we had to make God a priority, or God would slip from our lives. Similarly, after our children were born, we moved from one town to another and sought to join a parish. We knew that this was a crucial decision, because our children's faith lives would grow as a result of the kind of community we chose. Keeping God at the center of our week through regular attendance at Sunday Mass has nourished and shaped us, enabling us to keep God at the center of each day and each moment, moments so numerous and seemingly mundane that we are almost unaware that we are honoring our marriage and baptismal vows in those moments.

The most awe-inspiring expression of God's love in a marriage is the gift of children. Just as God's love was so great that it spilled over to us, so with the growth of a family, whether through natural birth or adoption, the married couple's love overflows and expands the circle of selfless love that begins in marriage. With the gift of children we learn even more fully how to surrender self-interest in order to serve the needs of the others in the family unit. Despite how tired we may be as parents, when the baby cries, we need to put the needs of another before our own. Self-sacrifice is evident in financial decisions to educate our children and provide them with enriching opportunities such as music lessons and scouting activities. This gift of our children has been a joy and a constant source of God's presence in our marriage. It is indeed humbling to hold a newborn in your arms and realize that your overwhelming love for this child is perhaps just a small manifestation of the infinite love that God offers to us, and gratitude overflows from the heart. Marriage and family are a very privileged place where this occurs.

Most wives and husbands at one time or another are jokingly told that their spouse is a "saint" to live with them. Saints lead us to God, and the spouse's primary vocation is to do just that: walk in God's light and lead one another to God. In this vein my husband is a saint, for he has shown me the face of God in more ways than I can count. I am indeed a much better Christian thanks to his role in my life. He was the first truly to teach me about what it would mean to live marriage as a sacrament. We became engaged over Thanksgiving break during our first year of graduate school, a year we were spending in cities located more than eight hundred miles apart. As we said goodbye at the airport at the conclusion of that Thanksgiving break, he expressed to me a feeling of nervousness about flying that he had not experienced before. When I asked him why he felt that way, he said, "Because what happens to me matters now. There is someone else who depends on me, who is affected by every choice I make, and whose happiness is more important than my own. The stakes are just so much higher now." With that simple statement of care and concern for me, he taught me an invaluable lesson about selfless love that mirrors Christ's love for us and that is the foundation upon which married love and family love are laid. Keeping this belief at the center of marriage is what makes us a sacramental people each and every day and makes that promised lifetime of marriage a blessing and a joy.

21. Faithful Love

MELINDA BROWN DONOVAN

"Love is patient; love is kind....It bears all things, believes all things, hopes all things, endures all things." So wrote Saint Paul in chapter 13 of his First Letter to the Corinthians. This year, as my parents celebrated their wedding anniversary, they lived out Saint Paul's words in a way that gave witness to the depth of their sacramental bond.

Elsie and Joe Brown are both ninety years old. They lived in their own home together in Topeka, Kansas, until October 2010, when Elsie's fragile mobility made it clear that Joe could not continue to care safely for her at home. She moved to a small care facility in their neighborhood, while Joe, fiercely independent, remained in their home. Joe's failing eyesight has left him legally blind, and lung disease requires him to use a portable oxygen unit at all times. Although this may sound like a frail person, he still mows his own lawn, tends his vegetable garden, and walks 0.6 miles to visit Elsie every day. When Joe makes these daily visits, they mostly hold hands, without a lot of talking, sometimes resting with their eyes closed. It is the comfort of human touch, the close physical proximity of the other, even for a short time, that sustains them.

In June 2011, their sixty-second wedding anniversary was fast approaching, and Joe wanted to honor the day in a special way. Normally, they have help with meals and cleaning; normally, my sister would have hosted them, but the usual supports were not available. Undaunted, Joe took things into his own hands and arranged for Elsie to be brought to their home—her first visit there since she had moved to the nursing home eight months earlier. He cleaned the house, cooked a roast-beef dinner, baked a loaf of fresh bread (with the help of his bread machine), and cut a rose from his garden for their table. After sharing this afternoon dinner together in their kitchen, Joe did the dishes while Elsie savored their memories as she browsed through old photo albums. Picture the tender love in this scene.

As my father recounted the events of the day to me, he was clearly delighted and proud of pulling off this wonderful surprise for his bride. But he also fretted about all the complications brought on by his failed eyesight: he dialed the driver four times before he got the right number; he couldn't tell what was clean and what wasn't; the thorns pricked him when he tried to cut the rose; he couldn't tell if the roast was done or not. "Love is patient… kind…bears all things…endures all things." Even with his frustration, he was clear: "It was all worth it, because I don't know how many more times I will have a chance to do it."

For me, the garden rose on the kitchen table symbolized the beauty and depth of their love in full bloom. The obstacles my father encountered seemed to confirm their covenant, which was sealed so long ago. This was a snapshot of what faithful, covenantal love looks like. This marriage relationship is a reflection of God's abundant, steadfast, faithful, and sacrificial love.

As events unfolded, this sixty-second wedding anniversary was indeed their last together in this life. With Joe at her side, Elsie passed into eternal life on December 27, 2011, shortly before this essay was published. Nine months later on September 28, 2012, Joe joined her. One rose was left blooming on their garden bush, which I cut for Joe's funeral. Their enduring love continues to define them and the way we remember them. Their ashes are buried together.

CONVERSATION QUESTIONS

1. Married love is a reflection of God's own love in the world. What have you learned about God's love from your marriage or other people's marriages? What particular aspects of marriage have taught you the most about God's love?

2. The nuptial blessing asks God to bless the couple so that their marriage might "enrich the Church." What are some important ways that marriages enrich the Church? What are some specific instances in your own life where marriage (either yours or someone else's) has helped build up your parish community?

3. It was stated that "vocations to ordained ministry are often portrayed as being more holy than other vocations." Do you feel that marriage is less sacred than ordained or consecrated life? Why or why not?

4. In considering the covenantal nature of marriage, what does the word *covenant* mean to you? How is it different from a contract?

5. How can you grow in your own married love or in supporting the married love of friends and family?

HOLY ORDERS

✝

1120 The ordained ministry or *ministerial* priesthood is at the service of the baptismal priesthood.[1] The ordained priesthood guarantees that it really is Christ who acts in the sacraments through the Holy Spirit for the Church. The saving mission entrusted by the Father to his incarnate Son was committed to the apostles and through them to their successors: they receive the Spirit of Jesus to act in his name and in his person [cf. John 20:21–23; Luke 24:47; Matt 28:18–20]. The ordained minister is the sacramental bond that ties the liturgical action to what the apostles said and did and, through them, to the words and actions of Christ, the source and foundation of the sacraments.

1547 The ministerial or hierarchical priesthood of bishops and priests, and the common priesthood of all the faithful participate, "each in its own proper way, in the one priesthood of Christ." While being "ordered one to another," they differ essentially.[2] In what sense? While the common priesthood of the faithful is exercised by the unfolding of baptismal grace—a life of faith, hope, and charity, a life according to the Spirit—the ministerial priesthood is

143

at the service of the common priesthood. It is directed at the unfolding of the baptismal grace of all Christians. The ministerial priesthood is a *means* by which Christ unceasingly builds up and leads his Church. For this reason it is transmitted by its own sacrament, the sacrament of Holy Orders.

1554 "The divinely instituted ecclesiastical ministry is exercised in different degrees by those who even from ancient times have been called bishops, priests, and deacons."[3] Catholic doctrine, expressed in the liturgy, the Magisterium, and the constant practice of the Church, recognizes that there are two degrees of ministerial participation in the priesthood of Christ: the episcopacy and the presbyterate. The diaconate is intended to help and serve them. For this reason the term *sacerdos* in current usage denotes bishops and priests but not deacons. Yet Catholic doctrine teaches that the degrees of priestly participation (episcopate and presbyterate) and the degree of service (diaconate) are all three conferred by a sacramental act called "ordination," that is, by the sacrament of Holy Orders:

> Let everyone revere the deacons as Jesus Christ, the bishop as the image of the Father, and the presbyters as the senate of God and the assembly of the apostles. For without them one cannot speak of the Church.[4]

ORDINATION EXAMINATIONS

EXAMINATION OF THE CANDIDATE FOR DEACON

The candidate then stands before the bishop who questions him:

> My son, before you are ordained a deacon, you must declare before the people your intention to undertake this office. Are you willing to be ordained for the

Church's ministry by the laying on of hands and the gift of the Holy Spirit?

The candidate answers: I am.

Bishop: Are you resolved to discharge the office of deacon with humility and love in order to assist the bishop and the priests and to serve the people of Christ?

Candidate: I am.

Bishop: Are you resolved to hold the mystery of the faith with a clear conscience as the Apostle urges, and to proclaim this faith in word and action as it is taught by the Gospel and the Church's tradition?

Candidate: I am.

Bishop: Are you resolved to maintain and deepen a spirit of prayer appropriate to your way of life and, in keeping with what is required of you, to celebrate faithfully the liturgy of the hours for the Church and for the whole world?

Candidate: I am.

Bishop: Are you resolved to shape your way of life always according to the example of Christ, whose body and blood you will give to the people?

Candidate: I am, with the help of God.

EXAMINATION OF THE CANDIDATE FOR PRIEST

The candidate then stands before the bishop who questions him:

My son, before you proceed to the order of the presbyterate, declare before the people your intention to undertake the priestly office. Are you resolved, with the help of the Holy Spirit, to discharge without fail the office of priesthood in the presbyteral order as a conscientious fellow worker with the bishops in caring for the Lord's flock?

The candidate answers: I am.

Bishop: Are you resolved to celebrate the mysteries of Christ faithfully and religiously as the Church has handed them down to us for the glory of God and the sanctification of Christ's people?

Candidate: I am.

Bishop: Are you resolved to hold the mystery of the faith with a clear conscience as the Apostle urges, and to proclaim this faith in word and action as it is taught by the Gospel and the Church's tradition?

Candidate: I am.

Bishop: Are you resolved to maintain and deepen a spirit of prayer appropriate to your way of life and, in keeping with what is required of you, to celebrate faithfully the liturgy of the hours for the Church and for the whole world?

Candidate: I am.

Bishop: Are you resolved to exercise the ministry of the word worthily and wisely, preaching the gospel and explaining the Catholic faith?

Candidate: I am.

Bishop: Are you resolved to consecrate your life to God for the salvation of his people, and to unite yourself more closely every day to Christ the High Priest, who offered himself for us to the Father as a perfect sacrifice?

Candidate: I am, with the help of God.

EXAMINATION OF THE CANDIDATE FOR BISHOP

The bishop-elect then rises and stands in front of the principal consecrator, who questions him: an age-old custom of the Fathers decrees that a bishop-elect is to be questioned before the people on his resolve to uphold the faith and to discharge his duties faithfully.

> My brother, are you resolved by the grace of the Holy Spirit to discharge to the end of your life the office of the apostles entrusted to us, which we now pass on to you by the laying on of hands?

The bishop-elect replies: I am

Principal consecrator: Are you resolved to be faithful and constant in proclaiming the Gospel of Christ?

Bishop-elect: I am.

Principal consecrator: Are you resolved to maintain the deposit of faith, entire and incorrupt, as handed down by the apostles and professed by the Church everywhere and at all times?

Bishop-elect: I am.

Principal consecrator: Are you resolved to build up the Church as the body of Christ and to remain united to it within the order of bishops under the authority of the successor of the apostle Peter?

Bishop-elect: I am.

Principal consecrator: Are you resolved to be faithful in your obedience to the successor of the apostle Peter?

Bishop-elect: I am.

Principal consecrator: Are you resolved as a devoted father to sustain the people of God and to guide them on the way of salvation in cooperation with the priests and deacons who share your ministry?

Bishop-elect: I am.

Principal consecrator: Are you resolved to show kindness and compassion in the name of the Lord to the poor and to strangers and to all who are in need?

Bishop-elect: I am.

Principal consecrator: Are you resolved as a good shepherd to seek out the sheep who stray and to gather them into the fold of the Lord?

Bishop-elect: I am.

Principal consecrator: Are you resolved to pray for the people of God without ceasing, and to carry out the duties of one who has the fullness of the priesthood so as to afford no grounds for reproach?

Bishop-elect: I am, with the help of God.

Principal consecrator: May God who has begun the good work in you bring it to fulfillment.

22. Ordained Ministry
A Brief History
SHARON L. MCMILLAN, SNDdeN

Deacons Ken, Mark, and Rubén stood at the beginning of the ordination rite on that bright, warm May morning and listened attentively as their vocation director put into words the desire of the entire local church: that these men be ordained to the responsibility of the priesthood. After the bishop consented and the assembly proclaimed its gratitude to God in enthusiastic words and applause, and after the bishop's homily, Ken, Mark, and Rubén stood again to promise fidelity to the demands of the priestly life they were about to begin.

The first question they heard offered a bit more precision to the meaning of priesthood. "Do you resolve, with the help of the Holy Spirit, to discharge without fail the office of priesthood in the presbyteral rank, as worthy fellow workers with the Order of Bishops in caring for the Lord's flock?" It is easy to miss the subtlety of that image; within the priesthood there are ranks, and these men are being ordained to the rank of presbyter identified in this promise as a fellow worker with the bishop.

During the ordination prayer itself, there is additional clarity. The bishop chanted, "And now we beseech you, Lord, in our weakness, to grant us these helpers that we need to exercise the priesthood that comes from the apostles. Grant, we pray, Almighty Father, to these, your servants, the dignity of the priesthood;…may they henceforth possess this office which comes from you, O God, and is next in rank to the office of bishop."

At the conclusion of the celebration, Fathers Ken, Mark, and Rubén were reminded of one more aspect of their priestly ministry as the bishop prayed in the final blessing, "May God make you true pastors who nourish the faithful with living bread and the word of life, that they may continue to grow into the one body of Christ."

PRESBYTERS AND THE BISHOP

It might come as a surprise to many in the parishes of Saint Paschal, Saint Louis Bertrand, and Holy Spirit who received these new priests to know that they are also called *presbyters*, and as presbyters are next in rank to the bishop (or, as the original source of the prayer has it, they hold "the office of second dignity"). They are not only his fellow workers but also share in the one ministerial priesthood with him. To hear them blessed as "true pastors" would be much more reassuring.

To have heard presbyters identified as "next in rank" to bishops, as possessing an office of "second dignity," and to find them actually addressed as priests (*sacerdos* in Latin) would have been a tremendous surprise to members of the Christian communities of the early centuries. As the late Sulpician scripture scholar Fr. Raymond Brown noted, the New Testament uses the title *presbyter-bishop* for those who exercised pastoral leadership over the community. In those days "presbyters and bishops were for all practical purposes the same" and "as a group they were responsible for the pastoral care of those churches."[1]

The apostles (such as Saint Paul) were the missionary figures who founded the local churches and then moved on. The presbyter-bishops were the residential figures who presided over the community and its life. But while they presided over communal worship as a central aspect of their leadership over the entire life of the community, and while these nascent Christian assemblies flourished in the vicinity of pagan priests and Jewish priests, no presbyter-bishops, no Christians, were ever given the title *priest* until the third century, and these were the bishops, not the presbyters.

David Power notes that the Letter to the Hebrews consoles those being persecuted for their discipleship in Christ with the knowledge that in him they have found the perfect and unique high priest, the one mediator necessary through whom full access to the Father is offered to all by his saving passion and resurrection. The First Letter of Peter teaches that Christ's disciples as a whole are a royal priesthood, anointed with Christ's own Spirit, offering spiritual sacrifices that are the gifts of their own lives. The crucified and risen Christ, then, continues to exercise his priestly ministry of praise and intercession before the Father surrounded by members of his Body, the priestly people who daily present their "bodies as a living sacrifice, holy and acceptable to God, which is (their) spiritual worship" (Rom 12:1). The shepherds who model and foster this discipleship are the presbyter-bishops, according to the descriptions in the New Testament.[2]

How is it that the Christian Church begins to distinguish bishops from its presbyters? How do the presbyters become characterized as holding an office of second rank? Why does the community begin to call its bishop a priest? And eventually, how does the strong collegial ministry of the presbyters give way to the individual identity of the person called a priest?

The writings of Saint Ignatius of Antioch demonstrate the first clear evidence of the existence of a separate and preeminent office of bishop.[3] He presides over the liturgical life of the community as a function of presiding over the community's life as a whole, but it is a service he undertakes in collaboration with the council of presbyters. By the third century, this model has become widely accepted: Christ, the high priest, animates each local community of priestly people led by one bishop (now also called a priest, *sacerdos*) together with a body of presbyters and another body of deacons.

AN ASSEMBLY OF MINISTRIES

But a wide variety of Spirit-inspired ministries flourished in the assemblies as well: widows, catechists, lectors, psalmists, acolytes, musicians, those offering direct service to the poor, to prisoners, to the hungry and homeless were some of the many specific roles among the priestly people. Thus, in a very real sense, the Church of the early centuries had no laity, that is, all the faithful were conscious of exercising Christ's priestly ministry through whichever charism they had received from the Spirit by their baptism. And bishops could speak to their parishioners out of similar convictions: "When I am frightened by what I am for you, then I am consoled by what I am with you. For you I am the bishop, with you I am a Christian. The first is an office, the second a grace; the first a danger, the second salvation (Saint Augustine, Sermon 340.1).[4] And also, "We are all one body, having such difference among ourselves as members with members, and (we) may not throw the whole upon the priests; but ourselves also so care for the whole church, as for a body common to us" (Saint John Chrysostom, Homily XVIII on Second Corinthians).[5]

Bishops exercise presidency, but it is a leadership set firmly within a collegial context.

THE RELATIONSHIP BETWEEN EUCHARIST AND COMMUNITY

The visual image of this model of community life is well reflected in what occurred within the eucharistic assembly. The bishop, as local pastor and president of the assembly, sat on the chair (the *cathedra*) in the center of the apse, surrounded by a semicircle of presbyters seated on a long, low bench, with the deacons standing nearby, ready to serve. Facing them and gathered before the altar were the baptized faithful, and in their midst was the reader, standing on a type of platform to give prominence to the proclamation of the scriptures. There was no one present who was not a member of an order in the church; from catechumens through the baptized faithful to the deacons, presbyters, and bishop, all knew themselves to be "ordained"/ordered within the assembly for the building up of the Body of Christ for the life of the world.

While the bishop ministered in the midst of the liturgical assembly in a very visible manner, the college of presbyters also participated actively in the rituals but in ways reserved to their order. Texts of the ancient *Apostolic Tradition* describe the presbyters as joining the bishop in the laying on of hands whenever that occurred, especially during the eucharistic prayer and during the ordination of presbyters. Saint Cyprian tells us they did the same whenever the bishop reconciled a penitent. They also had unique roles during baptism: anointing the elect with the oil of exorcism, performing the triple immersion, and anointing the newly baptized with the oil of thanksgiving before the bishop anointed them again (*Apostolic Tradition*, 21).

However, it was the bishop who was pastor and presider during these early centuries. Comparing the ordination prayer for a bishop makes the contrast clear: the only specific "spirit of grace and of counsel of the presbyterate" that is identified in their ordination prayer is that they may "help and govern your people with a pure heart," while the list of the bishop's responsibilities cited in the prayer at his ordination is extensive. He is "to feed your holy flock and to exercise the high priesthood,...to offer to you the holy gifts of your church,...to have power to forgive sins,...to loose every bond according to the power that you gave to the apostles...."[6] The bishop is at the head of the local church as teacher, shepherd, judge, and priest. He is also in communion with the other bishops and serves as the focus of unity for all the orders of the priestly people gathered around him.

THE IMPACT OF EXPANSION

This collegial model of ministry is short-lived; the Christian community expands and the need for new parishes (and thus new bishops) grows. Often during the third century, the solution was simply to elect and ordain more bishops from within their local communities. But in the fourth century—as the Church becomes first tolerated, then preferred, and finally elevated as the religion of the empire—the organic process of providing pastors for all the local communities cannot keep pace with the demand, especially in the outlying areas. The local bishop will then delegate his presbyters to take up the pastoral ministry in individual new parishes within the large urban areas as well as far out in the rural regions.

How significant it is that as they take up these individual pastoral and liturgical ministries, the presbyters need not undergo any further ordination. Each will become pastor as his own bishop is, but without any additional blessing for the substantially new roles of Word and Sacrament he will exercise. The venerable teaching of Tertullian, Cyprian, and the *Apostolic Tradition* (among others) holds true: presbyters were ordained into the same priesthood as the bishop.

As presbyters become individual pastors and learn to preside alone at the sacramental celebrations in their new parishes, the collegial reality of the local church begins to disintegrate. Certainly Christ, the high priest, still animates each local community of priestly people now led by one presbyter (soon also called a priest, *sacerdos*), but the presbyter is increasingly isolated from the bishop (with whom he often no longer lives, being so far away), isolated from the college of presbyters (ministering themselves in other distant parishes), and isolated from the college of deacons, who for the most part remain with the bishop in the city.

Imagine the sharp visual contrast of a celebration of the Eucharist at which one presbyter presides with the image of the collegial experience of Eucharist gathered around the bishop. In the presbyter's church there is not a bishop's *cathedra* in the center of the apse, nor is there any bench for the presbyters. (Eventually the altar will be moved into position against the wall.) The presbyter/priest in the new configuration may be assisted by one deacon or perhaps only one acolyte, a faint shadow of the earlier model rich with multiple and diverse liturgical ministries under the presidency of the bishop. It will be but a small step from this reduced image of the Eucharist to one in which the priest (all traces of a collegial presbyterate past) needs to assume by himself all liturgical ministries except acolyte as he celebrates the Eucharist alone at the altar facing the wall of the apse.

23. Presbyteral Identity within Parish Identity

SUSAN K. WOOD, SCL

Many baptized persons are called to give pastoral care in such roles as parish administrators, catechists, liturgical ministers, and directors of catechumenate programs. Many of them do so as professional ecclesial lay ministers. What distinguishes the ordained pastor from them is that, in the case of the ordained minister, the community elects this person for ordination by prayer to the Holy Spirit and the laying on of hands by the bishop to represent them in communions corresponding to the threefold office: communion of churches within a pastoral office; communion with Christ's self-offering within a prophetic office; and communion in apostolic faith within a prophetic office. The presbyter represents his people in the communion of churches through his participation in the priesthood of the bishop. He represents the ecclesial Body of Christ in Christ's eucharistic prayer to the Father and is able to represent Christ to his people in the sacraments. He exercises a prophetic office in proclaiming the faith of the apostolic church to this community. Ultimately, a presbyter's identity is defined representationally rather than functionally. His representational role is not limited to his priestly role within the Eucharist but extends to the rest of the threefold office. It is not simply a formal role but entails particular pastoral responsibilities.

Perhaps the most important role of ordained ministry is to assure the communion of a local community both with the apostolic tradition and with other eucharistic communities so that a local church is a communion in communion with other communions. We do not generally speak of presbyters as being in apostolic succession. The college of bishops is in succession to the apostolic college. Thus, the presbyter's claim as guarantor of apostolicity is tied to his relationship with his bishop. The presbyter extends the bishop's teaching role to the particular circumstances of the baptismal community that the presbyter serves.

The communion of churches is mediated by the communion of bishops. Parishes are united with this communion because of the relationship between priests and their bishop. Each particular church is defined as an altar community under the sacred ministry of the bishop. There can be no Eucharist apart from communion with other eucharistic communities. A Eucharist in isolation or division is a self-contradiction. Hence, ordination is more than a sacred power to confect the Eucharist; it is also the authorization through the election of the community, prayer to the Holy Spirit, and the laying on of hands to represent the community within the communion of churches.

The pastoral identity of the presbyter as pastor of a baptismal community includes the pastoral care of a church. Even though Roman Catholicism identifies the basic unit of the Church as the particular church under the ministry of the bishop, the particular church comes to event through the baptismal community of the parish. However, the difference between a particular church (the diocese) and a parish is that a parish cannot exist apart from its relationship to its bishop, who in turn represents the particular church in the communion of churches of the universal Church. A church cannot exist as Church in isolation. This communion is accomplished through the personal relationships of ordained presbyters to their bishops and of bishops to other bishops within the college of bishops. Ordination constitutes this network of relationships by authorizing a person to represent ecclesial communities in these relationships.

A parish does not include within itself everything needed to constitute a church, since it is lacking the ministry to represent it in the communion of particular churches. However, as we have seen, it does have ecclesial identity as long as it is in relationship with the rest of the particular church through the relationship of the presbyter to the local bishop. Here, a presbyter is defined not by what he does not represent, namely, the particular church, but by what he does represent, namely, the parish. As the parish has an ecclesial identity, so the presbyter finds his identity in relationship to this segment of the Church. He represents it and is the primary person responsible for its pastoral care. He has oversight of the various ministries within it.

As the person who is charged with the internal communion of the parish and its communion with the particular church, the presbyter presides over the sacrament of communion, the Eucharist. Presbyteral identity envisioned as a pastoral charge to a baptismal community is not in conflict with priestly identity within a eucharistic theology. Baptism and Eucharist celebrate the same mystery of Christ's dying and rising. What is celebrated once and for all in baptism is celebrated repeatedly in the Eucharist and in a sense is completed there, so there is a direct trajectory between the two sacraments. Conversely, what is celebrated in the Eucharist finds historical and particular expression in the everyday life of the baptismal community. This is the sense in which the Eucharist is the "source and summit" of the activity of the Church. The unity between the presbyter's pastoral identity and his priestly identity reflects the unity of these two sacraments.

A presbyter's role of pastoral leadership encompasses his priestly and prophetic roles but also includes the discernment and oversight of other ministries within the parish. A presbyter does not exercise pastoral leadership alone, but always collegially. This is not only the collegium of the presbyterate, but also the collegiality of shared ministry in a fully functioning baptismal community. A fully developed catechumenate implies a diversity and multiplicity of ministries and parish participation that extend far beyond liturgical ministries. Catechists, parish visitors, directors of faith formation, youth ministers, sponsors, those charged with sacramental preparation and hospitality all need direction, inspiration, and orchestration. All are necessary for evangelization, sacramental preparation, *mystagogia*, and the ongoing pastoral care of a congregation. Parishioners are not just consumers of these services, but actively participate in ministry, whether informally or formally, as lay ecclesial ministers. This is as it should be, for ministry and *diakonia* are attributes of the Church before they are attributes of an individual.

CONVERSATION QUESTIONS

1. In what ways do you think the ordained ministries (episcopate, presbyterate, and diaconate) are vital to today's Church? Do you believe that they are essential to the life of the Church?

2. What are some qualities of a good pastor? How might parishioners help their pastors cultivate these qualities?

3. How can parish communities help encourage vocations to ordained ministry?

4. What are your own best hopes for the future of ordained ministries in the Church?

5. How can you encourage vocations to lay ecclesial ministry?

CONCLUSION

✝

Sacraments
Visible Words of Friendship

DAVID FARINA TURNBLOOM

The sacraments are efficacious signs of grace, instituted by Christ and entrusted to the Church, by which divine life is [offered][1] to us. The visible rites by which the sacraments are celebrated signify and make present the graces proper to each sacrament. They bear fruit in those who receive them with the required dispositions (*Catechism of the Catholic Church* 1131).

Friendships need both words and actions. In order to share who we are with those we love, it is rarely enough to simply speak with them. We need to share experiences with friends (e.g., cooking a meal together, going for a hike, embracing one another, watching a film together, or exchanging gifts). Similarly, without conversation these actions can become superficial, making it difficult for our friendships to reach their true potential. For example, the flavor of a meal is almost always improved when seasoned with stories from a friend, and a film's beauty gains depth when seen through other viewpoints accessed through conversation. When friends want to share their lives with one another, they use a multitude of words and actions through which they simultaneously *give* friendship and *accept* friendship. The sacraments are rituals through which God offers us friendship. When words and actions

163

are united in the celebration of a sacrament, we experience what Saint Augustine called a "visible word." Through the celebration of each sacrament, God is speaking visible words of friendship.

THE SACRAMENTS REVEAL GOD

Whenever someone wants to know what the Second Vatican Council says about the sacraments, you can expect that they will begin by reading *Sacrosanctum Concilium* (The Constitution on the Sacred Liturgy). Indeed, regarding the sacramental life of the Church, it is arguably the most important text written in the last five hundred years. However, while often overlooked when it comes to sacramental theology, the Second Vatican Council's *Dei Verbum* (Dogmatic Constitution on Divine Revelation) offers a crucial insight into the nature of the sacraments: at their most fundamental level, the sacraments are divine revelation. In the following passage we see that the actions and words of God throughout history play a central role in the friendship offered to humankind.

> In His goodness and wisdom God chose to reveal Himself and to make known to us the hidden purpose of His will (see Eph 1:9) by which through Christ, the Word made flesh, man might in the Holy Spirit have access to the Father and come to share in the divine nature (see Eph 2:18; 2 Peter 1:4). Through this revelation, therefore, the invisible God (see Col 1:15; 1 Tim 1:17) out of the abundance of His love speaks to all men as friends (see Exod 33:11; John 15:14–15) and lives among them (see Bar 3:38), so that He may invite and take them into fellowship with Himself. This plan of revelation is realized by deeds and words having an inner unity: the deeds wrought by God in the history

of salvation manifest and confirm the teaching and realities signified by the words, while the words proclaim the deeds and clarify the mystery contained in them. (*Dei Verbum* 2)

God's revelation exists so that humankind might "come to share in the divine nature." As noted earlier, friendship is about sharing who you are with someone else. When we accept someone's friendship, that person becomes a part of who we are. Likewise, when God "takes us into fellowship with Himself," God becomes part of who we are. *Theosis, deification,* and *divinization* are all words that refer to this relationship whereby God offers humankind a share in divine life. The words and deeds of divine revelation are God's way of offering divine life to us so that "He may invite and take [us] into fellowship with Himself." The *Catechism of the Catholic Church* expresses the same idea differently when it says that the sacraments are signs "by which divine life is offered to us" (1131). So, if the words and deeds of divine revelation are the way that God has chosen to enter into friendship with us, those words and deeds demand further examination.

According to Christians, the most perfect form of divine revelation was Jesus of Nazareth. Through the inner unity of his deeds and words, humankind came to know God as a father who offers friendship, as *Abba.* In other words, Jesus Christ was the incarnate Word of God's friendship. Now that Jesus has ascended into heaven, the same divine revelation that was present through Jesus is present through the inner unity of the deeds and words that make up the sacraments—the sacraments are the visible words of divine friendship. When the *Catechism* says that the sacraments were instituted by Christ, it is attesting to this revelatory mission shared by both Christ and the sacraments. Jesus gave us the sacraments so that, through our liturgical celebrations, he might continue to reveal God to us throughout history. When he commands his disciples to "do this in remembrance of me," he is confronting us with an obligation. Our obligation to celebrate the sacraments is not simply a matter of God deserving our praise and thanksgiving. Rather, we are obligated to celebrate the sacraments because we need *to be* God's presence *to the world*. When we celebrate the sacraments, the revelation of God happens through our words and deeds.

INNER UNITY OF WORDS AND DEEDS

As *Dei Verbum* points out, the "plan of revelation is realized by deeds and words having an inner unity." Throughout this book we have printed the text of prayers used during the celebration of the sacraments. The words used are heavily rooted in the language of the scriptures. This is not an accident. The scriptures have a central role in the celebration of every sacrament.

Unfortunately, this fact is often forgotten. It is very common for us to make distinctions between the sacraments and the scriptures. Perhaps most notably, in the sacrament of reconciliation, we almost never turn our thoughts to the scriptures despite the fact that there are a great number of passages that might help us make better confessions. During this sacrament, we tend to separate our use of the scriptures from our sacramental actions. As you can see on page 96, the rubrics for the Rite of Penance makes a point of saying that the use of a scripture reading is optional. Even during the Eucharist, when the role of the scriptures is most apparent, there is a tendency to think of the Liturgy of the Word and the Liturgy of the Eucharist as two separate rituals instead of intimately connected parts of a single liturgy. When we hear the word *Eucharist*, too often we think only of the consecrated bread and wine. The words of the scriptures proclaimed and preached during our liturgies are the audible voice of God, who is also present through material and action. If these words aren't preached and heard, then the unity between deed and word suffers and the revelatory mission of the sacrament is hindered.

While the proclamation of the scriptures during our sacramental celebrations is vital, Saint Augustine calls the sacraments "visible words" because the word of God is not confined to the audible sounds of speech. In addition to the prayers we speak, the objects, sounds, gestures, postures, and smells that make up the sacraments all have meaning. As you can see in the text of the sacramental prayers, there is often a description of an action to be done by the person presiding. For example, during the Rite of Baptism the presider reaches out and touches the water as the blessing is said. The rubrics for each sacrament are filled with these prescriptions of actions and use of material. These signs are wrought with meaning, and as we have seen throughout this book, each deed speaks in its own manner. Being immersed in and pulled from water *speaks* about dying and rising in a way no spoken word ever could. The touch of a hand that anoints a sick body *speaks* about healing in a way that no "get well" wish could ever accomplish. However, in the celebration of the sacraments we are not left to choose between the verbal and the nonverbal. We are not forced to choose among our senses. Just as there is a unity among our senses, there is an inner unity between words and deeds. While it is a line used to reference marriage, it is good for anyone contemplating the words and deeds of the sacraments to remember the following: "What God has joined together, let no one separate."

REVEALING A FRIEND

The sacraments exist for the benefit of human beings. Throughout this book we have seen many ways that the sacraments benefit those who celebrate them. The sacraments of initiation give us new life; they strengthen us and bring us closer as a united Body of Christ. The sacraments of healing reconcile us to God and to one another by healing our bodies, minds, and spirits. Finally, the sacraments of vocation allow us to recognize and fulfill our roles in the Body of Christ. There is a traditional adage in Catholic sacramental theology: *Sacramenta sunt propter homines* (sacraments are for human beings). The sacraments are for our benefit. The sacraments are God's words and deeds present in our history. Through the sacraments God "speaks to all men as to friends and lives among them, so that He might invite and take them into fellowship with Himself." Through our worship, which (as the Common Preface IV tells us) is itself a gift from God, we are united to God in a communion of friendship. In each sacrament God comes to us as a friend. God is a friend who chooses us, who strengthens us, who unites us, who forgives us, who heals us, who is faithful to us, and who serves us. Through these visible words of friendship, we are offered divine life so that we might come to share in the divine nature. Simply put, through the sacraments we have God's life in our lives.

Acknowledgments

Excerpts from the English translation of *Rite of Baptism for Children* © 1969, International Commission on English in the Liturgy Corporation (ICEL); excerpts from the English translation of *Rite of Confirmation* © 1975, ICEL; excerpts from the English translation of *Rite of Penance* © 1974, ICEL; excerpts from *Documents on the Liturgy, 1963-1979: Conciliar, Papal, and Curial Texts* © 1982, ICEL; excerpts from the English translation of *Pastoral Care of the Sick: Rites of Anointing and Viaticum* © 1982, ICEL; excerpts from the English translation of *Rites of Ordination of a Bishop, of Priests, and of Deacons* © 2000, 2002, ICEL; excerpts from the English translation of *The Roman Missal* © 2010, ICEL. All rights reserved.

English translation of the *Catechism of the Catholic Church for the United States of America* copyright © 1994, United States Catholic Conference, Inc.—Libreria Editrice Vaticana. English translation of the *Catechism of the Catholic Church: Modifications from the Editio Typica* copyright © 1997, United States Catholic Conference, Inc.—Libreria Editrice Vaticana. All rights reserved. Used with permission.

"What Makes Us Catholic" excerpt from *What Makes Us Catholic: Eight Gifts for Life* [pages 2–3], copyright © 2002 by Thomas H. Groome. All rights reserved. Printed in the United States of America. HarperCollins Publishers, Inc. Used with permission.

"A Rite of Passage" reprinted from "The Three Days Parish Prayer in the Paschal Triduum" by Aidan Kavanagh in *A Rite of Passage* ©1992 Archdiocese of Chicago: Liturgy Training Publication 1-800-933-1800. www.LTP.org. All rights reserved. Used with permission.

"Baptizing a Child" reprinted from "Baptizing a Child: Whose Faith Formation Is It?" Mary Ann Clarahan in *The Furrow* 57, no. 1 (2006): 30–38. All rights reserved. Used with permission.

"Infant Baptism and Adult Faith" reprinted from "Infant Baptism and Adult Faith" by Michael Drumm, in *The Furrow* 44, no. 3 (1993): 131–39. All rights reserved. Used with permission.

CATHOLIC SACRAMENTS

"The Missionary Nature of Confirmation" reprinted from "The Missionary Nature of Confirmation" by Marc Caron in *Catechumenate: A Journal of Christian Initiation* 31, no. 6 © 2009 Archdiocese of Chicago: Liturgy Training Publication 1-800-933-1800. www.LTP.org. All rights reserved. Used with permission.

"The Sacrament of Marriage" by Michael G. Lawler and William P. Roberts, excerpt from *Christian Marriage and Family: Contemporary Theological and Pastoral Perspectives* copyright © 1996 by the Order of Saint Benedict, Inc. Published by Liturgical Press, Collegeville, Minnesota. All rights reserved. Used with permission.

"Ordained Ministry: A Brief History" by Sharon L. McMillan, S.N.D.de N. taken from *Celebrate!* March/April 2005. Louisville: Congregational Ministries Publishing. Used with permission.

"Presbyteral Identity within Parish Identity" by Susan K. Wood, excerpt from *Ordering the Baptismal Priesthood: Theologies of Lay and Ordained Ministry* edited by Susan K. Wood copyright © 2003 by the Order of Saint Benedict, Inc. Published by Liturgical Press, Collegeville, Minnesota. Reprinted with permission.

The following contributions were previously published in *C21 Resources* published by the Church in the 21st Century Center at Boston College:

"Anointed to Proclaim the Kingdom" by Liam Bergin. Reprinted with permission from the author.

"Eucharist: The Many-Faceted Jewel" by John F. Baldovin, S.J. Reprinted with permission from the author.

"Being Kept by the Eucharist" by Cardinal Sean Patrick O'Malley, O.F.M. Cap. Reprinted with permission from the Archdiocese of Boston Pastoral Center.

"The Ministries of the Eucharist" by Joyce Ann Zimmerman, C.PP.S. Reprinted with permission from the author.

"The Word in Worship" by Kathleen Hughes, RSCJ. Reprinted with permission from the author.

"Sacramental Real Presence" by Rodica Stoicoiu. Reprinted with permission from the author.

"The Feast of Corpus Christi" by Mark Ravizza, S.J. Reprinted with permission from the author.

"Why Go to Confession?" by John F. Baldovin, S.J. Reprinted with permission from the author.

"How to Go to Confession" by Kurt Stasiak, O.S.B. Reprinted with permission from the author.

Acknowledgments

"Anointing as Pastoral Sacrament" by Bruce T. Morrill, S.J. Reprinted with permission from the author.

"A Promised Lifetime" by Colleen Campion. Reprinted with permission from the author.

"Faithful Love" by Melinda Brown Donovan. Reprinted with permission from the author.

Notes

Part One: WHY THE SACRAMENTS?

1. Cf. *Sacrosanctum Concilium* 6; *Lumen Gentium* 2.
2. St. Leo the Great, *Sermo.* 74, 2: PL 54, 398.
3. St. Augustine, *De civ. Dei*, 22, 17: PL 41, 779; cf. St. Thomas Aquinas, *STh* III, 64, 2 *ad* 3.

Part Two: SACRAMENTS OF INITIATION

1. Paul VI, apostolic constitution, *Divinae Consortium Naturae*: AAS 63 (1971) 657; cf. RCIS Introduction 1–2.

BAPTISM

1. Cf. Council of Florence: DS 1314: *vitae spiritualis ianua.*
2. *Roman Catechism* II, 2, 5; cf. Council of Florence: DS 1314; CIC, can. 204, no. 1; 849; CCEO, can. 675, no. 1.

CONFIRMATION

1. Cf. *Lumen Gentium* 11.
2. Cf. Council of Florence (1439): DS 1319; *Lumen Gentium* 11; 12.
3. St. Ambrose, De myst. 7, 42: PL 16, 402–3.

Chapter 7. Anointed to Proclaim the Kingdom

1. Cf. Yves Congar, *I Believe in the Holy Spirit*, vol. 3 (New York: Seabury Press, 1983), 219; Congar, *The Word and the Spirit* (San Francisco: Harper and Row, 1986), 87.

2. Vatican II, *Apostolicam Actuositatem* (Decree on the Apostolate of Lay People) 3.

EUCHARIST

1. *Sacrosanctum Concilium* 47.

Chapter 8.
Eucharist: The Many-Faceted Jewel

1. "Baptism, Eucharist and Ministry" (Faith and Order Commission of the World Council of Churches, Lima, 1982). The commission included Avery Dulles, SJ, and Jean-Marie Tillard, OP. The main architect of the document was Professor Geoffrey Wainwright, formerly of Duke University, a British Methodist.

Chapter 11. The Word in Worship

1. *Sacrosanctum Concilium* 50, in *Documents on the Liturgy 1963–1979: Conciliar, Papal, and Curial Texts* (Collegeville, MN: The Liturgical Press, 1982).

2. *General Instruction of the Roman Mission* 46.

3. USCCB, "Preaching the Mystery of Faith: The Sunday Homily" (Washington, DC: United States Conference of Catholic Bishops, January 2013).

4. *Sacrosanctum Concilium* 51.

5. "Fulfilled in Your Hearing: The Homily in the Sunday Assembly" (Washington, DC: USCCB, 1982), 1.

6. *Lectio divina* is a pattern of studying a sacred text in progressively deeper ways: first, a close reading and rereading of the

passage; next, a time of meditation to go more deeply into the meaning of the passage; then, a time of prayer inspired by the text; and finally, a resting in contemplative silence.

7. The prologue of the *Rule* of Saint Benedict suggests this approach to *lectio*.

Chapter 12.
Sacramental Real Presence

1. Nathan Mitchell, *Real Presence: The Work of Eucharist* (Chicago: Liturgy Training Publications, 1998), 74.

2. Ibid., 75.

3. Ibid., 77.

4. David Power, *Mission, Ministry, Order: Reading the Tradition in the Present Context* (New York: Continuum, 2008), 326.

5. *Sacrosanctum Concilium* 7.

6. Mitchell, *Real Presence*, 99.

7. Ibid.

8. Power, *Mission, Ministry, Order*, 302.

9. Mitchell, *Real Presence*, 99.

10. Nathan Mitchell, *Cult and Controversy: The Worship of the Eucharist Outside of Mass* (New York: Pueblo Publishing Company, 1982), 148.

11. Ibid.

12. David Power, *The Eucharistic Mystery: Revitalizing the Tradition* (New York: Crossroad, 1992), 256.

13. Mitchell, *Real Presence*, 114.

14. Nathan Mitchell, *Meeting Mystery: Liturgy, Worship, Sacraments* (Maryknoll, NY: Orbis Books, 2006), 176.

15. Power, *The Eucharistic Mystery*, 319.

16. Mitchell, *Meeting Mystery*, 176.

Chapter 14. The Feast of Corpus Christi

1. Andre Dubus, "A Father's Story," in *Selected Stories*, 2nd ed. (New York: Vintage, 1995).

Part Three: SACRAMENTS OF HEALING
PENANCE

1. *Lumen Gentium* 11, para. 2.
2. OP 46: formula for absolution.

ANOINTING OF THE SICK

1. Council of Trent (1551): DS 1695; cf. Mark 6:13; Jas 5:14–15.

Chapter 17. The Richness of Tradition

1. Robert Taft, *Beyond East and West: Problems in Liturgical Understanding* (Washington, DC: Pastoral Press, 1984), 153.
2. *The Pastoral Care of the Sick* 6.

Chapter 18. Anointing as Pastoral Sacrament

1. *The Pastoral Care of the Sick* 149.

Part Four: SACRAMENTS OF VOCATION
MARRIAGE

1. CIC, can. 1055, no. 1; cf. *Gaudium et Spes* 48, para. 1.
2. Cf. *Sacrosanctum Concilium* 61.
3. Cf. *Lumen Gentium* 6.

HOLY ORDERS

1. Cf. *Lumen Gentium* 10, para. 2.
2. *Lumen Gentium* 10, para. 2.
3. Ibid., 28.
4. Saint Ignatius of Antioch, *Ad Trall.* 3, 1:SCh 10, 96.

Chapter 22. Ordained Ministry: A Brief History

1. Raymond Brown, *Priest and Bishop: Biblical Reflections* (New York: Paulist Press, 1970), 35.

2. David Power, "Priesthood Revisited: Mission and Ministries in the Royal Priesthood," in *Ordering the Baptismal Priesthood*, ed. Susan Wood (Collegeville: Liturgical Press, 2003), 87–120.

3. Paul Bradshaw, *Liturgical Presidency in the Early Church* (Bramcote, Nottinghamshire: Grove Books, 1983).

4. Translated by James Puglisi in his article "Presider as Alter Christus, Head of the Body?" *Liturgical Ministry* 10 (Summer 2001): 153–58.

5. Cited in Power, "Priesthood Revisited," 101.

6. The best translation of these texts is found in *The Apostolic Tradition*, ed. Paul Bradshaw, Maxwell Johnson, and L. Edward Phillips (Minneapolis: Fortress Press, 2002), 56 (for presbyters), 30 (for bishops).

CONCLUSION

Sacraments: Visible Words of Friendship

1. Editor's translation of the original Latin *praebetur*. The official English translation translates *praebetur* as "dispensed."

Contributors

John F. Baldovin, SJ, is a professor of historical and liturgical theology at Boston College School of Theology and Ministry.

Liam Bergin has been a priest-in-residence at Gate of Heaven and Saint Brigid Parishes in South Boston, Massachusetts, since May 2012. He is professor of the practice in the Theology Department at Boston College. A native of Ireland, he studied and taught in Italy for twenty-four years and served as rector of the Pontifical Irish College in Rome for ten years. During this time, he was also a professor at the Pontifical Gregorian University, where he had earned a doctorate in sacred theology.

Colleen Campion is the liturgy director at St. Timothy Catholic Church in Norwood, Massachusetts. She is a wife of twenty-six years and the mother of four children. She is a candidate for a master's degree in pastoral ministry at the School of Theology and Ministry at Boston College.

Marc B. Caron completed his seminary studies at the Catholic University of America in Washington, D.C. He served as one of the chancellors of the Roman Catholic Diocese of Portland and as director of the Department of Ministerial Services for the diocese. At the diocesan level, he is a member of the Presbyteral Council, the College of Consultors, the Priests' Personnel Board, and the Liturgical Commission.

Mary Ann Clarahan is a member of the Sisters of Mercy of the Americas. She is currently teaching in Rome at Beda College and the Gregorian University.

Melinda Brown Donovan is associate director of continuing education at the School of Theology and Ministry at Boston College.

Michael Drumm is a priest of the diocese of Elphin and teaches theology at Mater Dei Institute, Drumcondra, in Dublin, Ireland.

Kathleen Hughes, RSCJ, is former professor in the Department of Word and Worship at Catholic Theological Union, Chicago, and former provincial of the United States Province of the Society of the Sacred Heart. She was the first woman to receive a doctorate in liturgical studies from the University of Notre Dame.

Thomas H. Groome is a professor of theology and religious education at Boston College and the director of the Church in the 21st Century Center.

Aidan J. Kavanagh, OSB (1929–2006), was professor emeritus of liturgics at the Yale Institute of Sacred Music and Yale Divinity School. He served as acting director of the Institute and acting dean at Yale Divinity School, the first Roman Catholic priest to lead the School.

Chelsea King holds a bachelor's degree in philosophy and theology from the University of Notre Dame. She completed her master's degree in theological studies at the School of Theology and Ministry at Boston College where she is now undergoing her second master of theology degree.

The Rev. Dr. Lizette Larson-Miller is Professor and Huron-Lawson Chair in Moral & Pastoral Theology in the Faculty of Theology at Huron University College, London, Ontario.

Michael G. Lawler is professor of theology and dean of the graduate school at Creighton University. His works have been published widely in theological journals in the United States and Europe, and he is the author of numerous books.

Contributors

Sharon L. McMillan, SNDdeN, is a Sister of Notre Dame de Namur and received her doctorate from the Pontifical Liturgical Institute at Sant'Anselmo, Rome.

Bruce T. Morrill, SJ, is the Edward A. Malloy Professor of Catholic Studies at Vanderbilt University.

Cardinal Seán Patrick O'Malley, OFM Cap, has served as Archbishop of Boston since 2003. He was elevated to the cardinalate in 2006 by Pope Benedict XVI. Cardinal O'Malley is a member of the Order of Friars Minor Capuchin. Since his ordination to the episcopacy on August 2, 1984, he has served as the Bishop of the dioceses of St. Thomas in the Virgin Islands; Fall River, Massachusetts; and Palm Beach, Florida.

Mark Ravizza, SJ, is an associate professor at Santa Clara University. In addition to his work in the Department of Philosophy, Mark is a senior fellow of the Bannan Institute for Jesuit Education and Christian Values. He earned his doctorate from Yale University.

William P. Roberts is professor of theology at the University of Dayton and the author of several books. He has chaired two national symposia, "Marriage and The Catholic Church: A Contemporary Evaluation," and "Divorce and Remarriage: Religious and Psychological Perspectives."

Kurt Stasiak, OSB, is a monk of Saint Meinrad Archabbey and the director of Spiritual Formation for the School of Theology. Father Kurt is the author of several books and has published numerous articles and book reviews appearing in a variety of publications.

Rodica Stoicoiu is a professor in the theology department at Mount St. Mary's University in Emmitsburg, Maryland.

David Farina Turnbloom is an assistant professor of theology at the University of Portland. He received his doctorate from Boston

College where he specialized in liturgical theology and theological ethics.

Susan K. Wood, SCL, a Sister of Charity of Leavenworth, Kansas, is professor of systematic theology in the Department of Theology at Marquette University. She is an associate editor of *Pro Ecclesia* and serves on the editorial advisory board of the journal *Ecclesiology*. Most of her writing explores the connections between ecclesiology and sacramental theology.

Joyce Ann Zimmerman, CPPS, is the director of the Institute for Liturgical Ministry at Dayton, Ohio; the founding editor of Liturgical Ministry; and the vice president of the North American Academy of Liturgy.

C21   BOSTON COLLEGE

THE CHURCH IN THE 21ST CENTURY CENTER

The Church in the 21st Century Center at Boston College offers dynamic programming publications, and web and digital media materials to be a catalyst and resource for the renewal of the Catholic Church. www.bc.edu/church21